JANE AUSTEN'S
'SIR CHARLES GRANDISON'

JANE AUSTEN'S

'SIR CHARLES GRANDISON'

*

Transcribed and Edited by
BRIAN SOUTHAM

Foreword by
LORD DAVID CECIL

OXFORD · AT THE CLARENDON PRESS
1980

Oxford University Press, Walton Street, Oxford OX2 6DP

London Glasgow New York Toronto
Delhi Bombay Calcutta Madras Karachi
Kuala Lumpur Singapore Hong Kong Tokyo
Nairobi Dar es Salaam Cape Town
Melbourne Wellington
and associate companies in
Beirut Berlin Ibadan Mexico City

Published in the United States by
Oxford University Press, New York

British Library cataloguing in Publication Data
Austen, Jane
Jane Austen's 'Sir Charles Grandison'
I. Southam, Brian Charles   II. Sir Charles Grandison
822'.7   PR4034.S/   80-40467
ISBN 0-19-812637-9

Printed in Great Britain
at the University Press, Oxford
by Eric Buckley
Printer to the University

CONTENTS

FOREWORD

BY LORD DAVID CECIL

Admirably edited and annotated by Mr Southam, here is Jane
Austen's only surviving attempt to write a play of any length;
a light-hearted dramatization of some scenes from Samuel
Richardson's novel, *Sir Charles Grandison*. Though carefully
preserved by the Austen family for over one hundred and fifty
years, it has never before been published. Mr Southam tells us
why. According to a family tradition, Jane Austen was not its
author: it was dictated to her by her niece Anna (daughter of her
eldest brother James), when a child. Mr Southam gives us
reasons for disbelieving this tradition. The early scenes of the
play appear to have been written before Anna was born and the
later scenes, when she was, at most seven years old—though
already, it seems, an enthusiastic admirer of Sir Charles
Grandison. It is odd enough that at so early an age she should
have read and enjoyed a novel for grown-up people in seven
volumes and largely made up of solemn moralizing, diversified
from time to time by scenes of attempted seduction or exhibiting
a heroine afflicted by fits of melancholy madness. It is surely
incredible that the same little girl should have been capable of
the sustained literary effort involved in dramatizing them; all the
more because this is done in a spirit of satirical burlesque
intentionally unlike that of the book on which it is founded. The
probability, Mr Southam concludes, is that Jane Austen started
the play as a brief skit but laid it aside. A few years later she took
it up again with a view to turning it into a play for family
performance; but, for reasons unknown, discarded it again
before she had properly finished it. However, while still engaged
on its later scenes, she showed it to her little niece with whom she

was very friendly, asked her for suggestions; and sometimes took them. From this grew up the tradition that Anna was the author of the work and her Aunt Jane only its amanuensis.

To read the text is to understand why this tradition was easily accepted. Beyond the fact that the first few scenes are a little like some of the skits she wrote as a teenager, it is not characteristic of Jane Austen. In its unfinished form it is too scrappy and incoherent and lacking in her sharp-edged precision of style. Were it not written in her elegant flowing, eighteenth-century hand, I doubt if one would think it to be hers. My guess is that she wrote it at odd moments and in a hurry; and perhaps to please Anna rather than herself. I can fancy Anna asking 'Do go on with the play about Sir Charles Grandison, Aunt Jane': and Aunt Jane dropping whatever she was doing, quickly to improvise a speech to be added to the manuscript.

Indeed if it does not much increase our appreciation of Jane Austen the artist, the play enriches our knowledge of Jane Austen, the member of a family. During the time she wrote it, her father was still Rector of Steventon and family life there in full swing, a life 'made pleasant' we are told 'by all the fun and nonsense of a large and clever family'. Cleverness and a sense of fun found expression in a number of ways; parlour games, charades, theatricals, and above all, writing. This seems to have been generally in a light vein—parodies, skits, satirical sketches in prose or verse. Mrs Austen was noted for her humorous verses; as an Oxford undergraduate, James Austen started a lively magazine called *The Loiterer*; most of his brothers and sisters went in for authorship of some kind. Jane Austen was only one member of a family of authors. She differed from the majority of great writers in that she embarked on a literary career less as a means of self-expression than as a way to contribute to home entertainment. She started young. By her early teens she already spent much of her time writing. Too much, she lamented, in later life; she said she regretted that she had not occupied herself in improving her mind by studying. In this she was mistaken. Jane Austen's mind was in no need of improvement.

By the time she had started on the later and larger instalment of 'Sir Charles Grandison', she had grown up and a new generation of relations were asking to be entertained. Jane Austen was ready and glad to gratify their request; for the new generation of Austens were coming to be important figures in her life and a chief source of her pleasure in it. Jane Austen was a born aunt; the most active and successful aunt in our literary history. On the one hand she delighted in the company of young people of any age and had an unusual gift for pleasing them; on the other hand, her strong family feeling led her to prefer those young people who were related to her. Finally, childless herself, she had enough unsatisfied maternal instinct to make her take a peculiar interest in the children of others. Two or three of these became special favourites: among them was Anna; for Anna shared her tastes. Anna was literary. As a very little girl she listened enthralled to Aunt Jane telling her fairy stories of her own invention. Later it was her turn to tell stories to Aunt Jane who listened appreciatively. Years later Anna began a novel which was sent in instalments to Aunt Jane for advice. Aunt Jane was delighted to give it, but spoke to her niece as an equal whose words were not to be taken too reverently. 'If you think differently, do not mind me'—so she ends one paragraph of advice. I imagine that it was already in this relaxed and equal tone that she conversed with little Anna as they 'collaborated' in the dramatization of *Sir Charles Grandison*.

All the more because they both enjoyed the book so much. As Mr Southam reminds us, it is said to have been Jane Austen's favourite novel. I confess that this surprises me: I find the book now and again absurd and at all times long-winded: I cannot help sympathizing a little with Miss Andrews in *Northanger Abbey*

[ix]

who could not get beyond the first volume. However I expect that both of us are wrong. Certainly we have distinguished opinion against us; George Eliot enjoyed *Sir Charles Grandison* almost as much as Jane Austen did. No doubt both authoresses were impressed by Richardson's strange power to compel the reader to believe in his fictional world and even more by his extraordinary insight into the workings of the feminine heart. Further, this particular book of his would have had a special appeal to Jane Austen as a pioneer example of the social-domestic type of novel which she was to write herself.

Yet her admiration for *Sir Charles Grandison* did not stop her from noting its occasional absurdity. Once again we are reminded that Jane Austen's sense of the ridiculous, unsleeping and irrepressible, was the outstanding characteristic of her genius, the primary source of her inspiration. Nor could admiration, however enthusiastic, check its activity. On the contrary, she got a mischievous pleasure out of laughing at what she also looked up to. As a girl of fifteen reading history, she made rollicking fun out of the romantic sentiment stirred in her by the figure of Mary Queen of Scots. It is similarly typical of her that her only known attempt at sustained playwriting should be a burlesque of a much-loved and serious novel.

PREFACE

Jane Austen's 'Sir Charles Grandison' is presented here for the first time and it has seemed right to try to meet the needs and interests of different readers—the scholars and experts as well as those who read Jane Austen purely for pleasure. Those whose prime interest is in reading the play as a play will want to turn first to the text which has been edited with that purpose in view.

For those who want to examine the original manuscript as closely as possible, there is a full transcription with a commentary upon the changes and cancellations. Students of literature will want to explore the relationship between the play and Richardson's novel, so there are detailed notes on Jane Austen's use of *The History of Sir Charles Grandison*.

In the Introduction I have set out to explain how it is, at this late date, that we come to be looking at a newly discovered work by Jane Austen. This takes us into the history of the Austen family; properly so, since 'Grandison' is closely involved with the family life of the Austens, their literary enthusiasms and activities. These are domestic matters. But they also have some bearing upon Jane Austen's development as a novelist and I have tried to set the play in a reasonably broad perspective.

ACKNOWLEDGEMENTS

In the preparation of this edition, I have been helped by a number of people and I would like to record my gratitude and thanks for particular assistance to Professor Daniel Waley, Keeper of the Department of Manuscripts at the British Library, Mr David Gilson, Miss Helen Lefroy, Lt.-Commander Francis Austen RN Rtd., Marquess Conyngham, and Dr Roger Fiske.

For the text of *Sir Charles Grandison* I have used the Oxford English Novels edition, 1972, edited by Jocelyn Harris.

LIST OF PLATES

INTRODUCTION

'There would be more genuine rejoicing at the discovery of a complete new novel by Jane Austen than any other literary discovery, short of a new play by Shakespeare, that one can imagine.' Margaret Drabble's words in the Introduction to the Penguin edition of *Lady Susan*, *The Watsons*, and *Sanditon*, published in 1974 were followed three years later, in the autumn of 1977, by a Jane Austen discovery, not of that magnitude, not 'a complete new novel', but something equally unexpected, 'Sir Charles Grandison', a new play. If it was not greeted with a burst of 'rejoicing', it was certainly met with considerable interest and curiosity. Jane Austen as playwright was an intriguing idea. The novels already so dramatic, their dialogue and characters so vivid and unforgettable, what new facet of her genius was to be revealed? Then there was the literary reference in the title. What could be the connection—an extraordinary one, at the very least—between this fifty-two-page play and *The History of Sir Charles Grandison*, the novel by Samuel Richardson, published in 1753 and 1754, seven volumes long? And bibliographers remarked on the total unexpectedness of the find. The surviving manuscripts have been so carefully preserved, so scrupulously recorded, and so meticulously edited, that it seemed virtually impossible that anything from Jane Austen's pen, however slight, could have remained unknown into the late 1970s.

In the pages that follow, I have tried to reconstruct the history of the manuscript in order to explain the mystery of its sudden and belated appearance. In this enquiry, as with other puzzles that arise in the manuscript, the physical appearance of the pages tells us a good deal; so does the style of the handwriting and the pattern of revisions and changes, sometimes in Jane Austen's hand, sometimes not, sometimes in ink, elsewhere in pencil. Quite apart from matters of antiquarian or bibliographical interest, then, it is important that readers are able to look at the facsimile for themselves. Some of the suggestions offered here are tentative, certainly not conclusive. With the facsimile in front of them individual readers can arrive at their own explanations— why, for example, the title-page announces the play to be in six acts, while the play itself comes to a close quite naturally at the end of Act Five, to the decisive stage-direction, 'The Curtain Falls'; why, in Act One, we go straight from Scene One to Scene Three, when there are no pages missing from the manuscript to explain the absence of Scene Two; why some of the most amusing lines of the play—in the middle of the marriage ceremony, on page sixteen of the manuscript—were crossed out, apparently by Jane Austen.

If these are practical reasons for consulting the manuscript, there is also the strong human interest of looking behind the printed pages of a great writer. Whether we turn to the manuscript out of mere curiosity or sentiment or, as students, to check a point of detail, we are inevitably brought closer to the author herself, to the act of writing and the process of creation. No amount of commentary and description can ever replace seeing the actual manuscript for oneself; and in this respect the facsimile stands as a workable substitute. Although of course it cannot convey the feel of the original, the texture of the paper, and so on, none the less, the facsimile does reveal essential features, such as its scrappiness and untidiness and the changes in the handwriting that show it to have been written over a period of years. Jane Austen's other manuscripts, even the first drafts, are unlike 'Grandison' in this regard. However heavily corrected they may be, they are neither scrappy nor untidy. In appearance, their pages are usually neat and careful, the lines regularly spaced. 'Grandison' is different; and it is a difference that helps us to understand the nature of the play as a piece of home entertainment, dashed off to amuse the family, begun in the early 1790s, put aside for some years and then finished about 1800.

It follows from this that we are certainly not dealing with the vintage Jane Austen. 'Grandison' is amusing enough and highly performable, but no masterpiece, not even a minor masterpiece. This is a qualification that means something, since at least two of the early works, 'Love and Friendship', written in 1790, and 'The History of England', completed in November 1791, fall into the 'minor masterpiece' category. Their comedy is hilarious, their satire deadly accurate. Perfect of their kind, they are enjoyable to this day. Whereas 'Grandison' is very uneven, often juvenile. It has no memorable characters, and few moments of high comedy or flashes of living dialogue. So anyone who comes to 'Grandison' hoping to find a new Jane Austen—Jane Austen the dramatist—is bound for disappointment.

None the less, the play does make a fascinating addition to the collection of minor works. It takes us into Jane Austen's private writing, the pieces that she set down not with any thought of publication but simply to please herself and entertain the family. It also serves to remind us of the strongly dramatic vein in the novels. Perhaps most important of all, for the literary historian, it adds considerably to our understanding of Jane Austen's experience of Richardson. It has long been known to us that Richardson was her favourite novelist, and *Grandison* her favourite novel, its characters 'as well remembered as if they had been living friends'.[1] *Grandison* pervades her mature writing, sometimes obviously, in details of character or scenes that seem to have been taken from the novel and adjusted to suit her own purposes; sometimes more fleetingly, in a closeness of tone or feeling. And it was from *Grandison*, above all, that Jane Austen learned how to develop her own personal style of social comedy—*domestic* social comedy, closely and realistically observed, from the woman's point of view.

The 'discovery' of 'Grandison' should properly stand in inverted commas. Strictly speaking, it would be more correct to refer to its emergence in 1977 as a *re*-discovery, following a re-attribution. Within one branch of the Austen family—the descendants of Jane's eldest brother, James—the play was common knowledge. The manuscript had been in their possession since the time of Jane Austen's death in 1817 and was handed down from generation to generation, a precious memento of Aunt Jane. The other surviving manuscripts were gradually made public—a process that began in 1871 when some small items and extracts were added to the second enlarged edition of the *Memoir*;[2] and continued in the sequence of full and authoritative texts edited by R. W. Chapman and published by the Oxford University Press between 1923 and 1954. But 'Grandison' was passed by. For although the handwriting of the manuscript was unmistakably Jane Austen's, according to family tradition the play was not in fact by her. It was said to be the work of her favourite niece Jane Anna Elizabeth Austen, the eldest child of James Austen. Anna was born on 15 April 1793, married Benjamin Lefroy in 1814, and died on 1 September 1872.

At some time in the 1940s this attribution was written down and attached to the manuscript by its then owner, Miss Louie Langlois Lefroy, a granddaughter of Anna Austen. Miss Lefroy placed 'Grandison' in an envelope with other Austen papers, identifying the contents with this note:

> Copy of letter from Jane Austen
> Recollections of Jane Austen by her
> niece "Anna" Lefroy (née Austen
> written I believe for her half brother
> J E Austen Leigh's memoir of his Aunt.
> Also a play of "Anna's" when a child
> written out for her, by her Aunt "Jane
> Austen".

(For the wording of this note I am grateful to Lt.-Commander Francis Austen.) Miss Helen Lefroy identifies the hand as that of her godmother and believes that the note was probably written when Louie Lefroy was going through the papers inherited from her sister Jessie, in 1941. Louie Lefroy died in 1954, at the age of ninety.

As far as we can trace it, the tradition of 'Grandison's' authorship comes from the third of Anna Austen's six daughters, Fanny Caroline Lefroy. It was first made public in *Jane Austen: Her Homes and Her Friends* by Constance Hill, published in 1902. Miss Hill gives a direct quotation from Fanny Lefroy's reminiscences: 'I have still in my possession, in Aunt Jane's writing, a drama my mother dictated to her, founded on *Sir Charles Grandison*, a book with which she was familiar at seven years old.'[3]

This statement was never questioned, within the family or outside. There was no reason why it should be, coming as it did from a source so impeccable and declared so straightforwardly and circumstantially. All that is known about Anna Austen's early life confirms its possibility. Her mother, Anna Austen, died in May 1795, at the village of Deane in Hampshire, where James was curate. At the time, Anna was only just two. She was so distressed that her father sent her to Steventon, one and a half miles away, to be cared for by her aunts Jane and Cassandra. This was the period when Jane Austen was making a start on the earliest of the six novels.

Following that first visit in the spring of 1795, Anna was to become a frequent guest at Steventon Rectory. She attached herself to her aunt Jane, who allowed the little girl into her sanctum, the dressing-room where she carried on her writing in strict privacy. In this way, Anna came to know of the early novels, at a time when they were being kept from the rest of the family. This had its embarrassments. There was one occasion when Anna, 'a very intelligent, quick-witted child', overheard Jane reading the original draft of *Pride and Prejudice* to Cassandra; 'she caught up the names of the characters and repeated them so much downstairs that she had to be checked; for the composition of the story was still a secret kept from the knowledge of the elders.'[4] The first version of *Pride and Prejudice* was written between October 1796 and August 1797. So Anna must have been a highly retentive and parroting four- or five-year-old— just as she would need to be, at the age of seven, to compose in her head a play based upon *Sir Charles Grandison*.

The other parts of Fanny Lefroy's statement also ring true. By all accounts, Jane Austen was a perfect aunt. She gave up a good deal of her precious time and energy in helping her young nephews and nieces with their own writing. So it would have been completely in character for her to have encouraged Anna by writing out the play; and *Grandison* could very well have been the model, since it was so much a favourite with her aunt and a source for what Anna remembered as 'the flow of native wit, with all the fun and nonsense of a large and clever family.'[5] Jane Austen had already poked fun at *Grandison* in some of her childhood satires[6] and these Anna would have heard read aloud in the family circle. And we know something of Anna's own creative gift from an earlier sentence in Fanny Lefroy's recollections: 'To my mother she was especially kind, writing for her the stories she invented for herself long ere she could write, and telling her others of endless adventure and fun, which were carried on from day to day, or from visit to visit!'[7] Thus, it is said, 'Sir Charles Grandison' came into existence.

Among the Austens, Anna was regarded as something of a writer. In 1814, just before her marriage, she was at work on a novel entitled 'Which is the heroine?', sending the instalments of the story to her aunt for comment and advice; and thanks to these writing ambitions we have the small and precious group of letters in which Jane Austen comments on the art of fiction.[8] It was in recognition of this close literary relationship that Anna was given the manuscripts of *The Watsons*, *Sanditon*, and the two cancelled chapters of *Persuasion* after her aunt's death, in July 1817. *Sanditon* was Jane Austen's last, uncompleted novel and Anna added a continuation.[9] This was never published. But she did get into print, modestly, with two children's books, *The Winter's Tale* (1841) and *Springtide* (1842); and she was probably the author of a short story that appeared in the *Literary Souvenir* for 1834, described as being 'By a niece of the late Miss Austen'.[10]

So within the family the tradition of Anna's 'Grandison' authorship was never in doubt. Outside the family, it remained unquestioned because it was not widely known—at least, going by the fact that no Jane Austen scholar, not even Dr Chapman himself, seems to have been sufficiently interested or curious to enquire further into Fanny Lefroy's statement,[11] even though it was repeated by Mary Augusta Austen-Leigh (the daughter of James Edward Austen-Leigh, the author of the *Memoir*). In *Personal Aspects of Jane Austen* (1920), she was able to add the information that the manuscript 'still exists'.[12] While the known manuscripts of Jane Austen were gradually shepherded towards publication, 'Grandison' remained out of sight. It was not shown to Dr Chapman when he made his round of the Austen papers in the 1920s and 1930s. Louie Lefroy and her sister Isabel, who lived together in the Hampshire village of Crondall, gave Chapman a great deal of help and access to their share of the family papers. Their house was something of a Jane Austen shrine. Their sister Jessie, who had the 'Grandison' manuscript, was no less proud of the family connection. But she lived separately in Winchester. As Helen Lefroy remembers her, Jessie 'was an independent person of magical charm and kindness; and it would be wholly in keeping with my memory of her that she went her own way, more concerned about people than about papers, and did not want advice from R. W. C. or his curiosity.'[13]

In the late 1950s and early 1960s, I was myself working on a study of Jane Austen's literary manuscripts. But I saw no reason then to seek out the 'Grandison' manuscript. I accepted Fanny Lefroy's statement at face value and merely referred to the play unseen as evidence of the younger Austens continuing familiarity with Richardson's novel.[14]

As far as I can discover, prior to Autumn 1977 'Grandison' had been seen by no one outside the family other than the auctioneers and officials of the British Library. Until it was studied closely, in preparing the entry for the auction catalogue,[15] those who knew about the manuscript supposed that its importance was as a holograph, and no more, in Jane Austen's hand. As a composition of Anna Austen, its literary and historical importance was negligible; its value, a very high commercial value, was wholly as a Jane Austen autograph.

As long as nothing was known about the size and precise character of 'Grandison', there was no reason to doubt the story of Anna's authorship. Everything points in its favour. My own assumption had been that 'Grandison' was no more than a trifle, a few pages long, simply a piece of childish fun, put together from the *Grandison* jokes that peppered the conversation at Steventon. I supposed it to be similar to the little joke-playlets that Jane Austen had written a few years earlier.[16] These are amusing scraps, two or three pages long, which Anna could have imitated without difficulty, given some encouragement and prompting from her aunt.

But as soon as we have the manuscript in front of us, this line of speculation is brought to a halt. 'Grandison' is over fifty pages long. For all its light-heartedness and absurdity, it bears the stamp of an adult mind. Can we really suppose that a child of

seven, too young to write out the play for herself, who had to
depend on her aunt as copyist, was capable not just of composing
such a work but of composing it in her head? If 'Grandison' was
written later than 1800, when Anna might have been old enough
to conceive the play, Jane Austen would have had no hand in it.
At that age the girl could have written it out for herself.

Taken together, the literary evidence and the chronological
circumstances point quite clearly to Jane Austen as the play's
author. The manuscript itself provides more evidence. While the
paper used for the later sections is watermarked 1796 and 1799,
and the style of the handwriting looks right for a date around
1800, the handwriting of the opening section, comprising the
whole of Act One, on undated paper, is much less formed, less
mature. These pages were written some years earlier, possibly
before Anna was born. This local 'technical' evidence is again
supported by the 'literary': for Act One is much less amusing
than the rest of the play, much less accomplished dramatically.
It could well belong to the early 1790s, when Jane Austen was
first trying her hand at *Grandison* jokes in the small prose satires.

Within the family, Jane Austen's devotion to *Grandison* was a
legend in itself. According to the *Memoir*, 'Her knowledge of
Richardson's works was such as no one is likely again to acquire
. . . Every circumstance narrated in Sir Charles Grandison, all
that was ever said or done in the cedar parlour, was familiar to
her; and the wedding days of Lady L. and Lady G. were as well
remembered as if they had been living friends.'[17] Her brother
Henry Austen reported that she was in the habit of recalling the
very day of the year upon which episodes in the novel were
supposed to have taken place.[18] In the 'Biographical Notice'
that Henry wrote after his sister's death, *Grandison* is picked out,
the only novel to be mentioned by name:

It is difficult to say at what age she was not intimately acquainted with
the merits and defects of the best essays and novels in the English

language. Richardson's power of creating, and preserving the consistency of his characters, as particularly exemplified in *Sir Charles Grandison*, gratified the natural discrimination of her mind, whilst her taste secured her from the errors of his prolix style and tedious narrative. She did not rank any work of Fielding quite so high. Without the slightest affectation she recoiled from every thing gross. Neither nature, wit, nor humour, could make her amends for so very low a scale of morals.[19]

Henry's opening words sound like nothing more than literary flourish, an eloquent obituaryism. But like the claim in the *Memoir* as to Jane Austen's verbatim knowledge of *Grandison*, this claim, too, is not a piece of empty rhetoric. Jane Austen's knowledge of the novel did indeed date from childhood, possibly from the earliest moment that she was able to tackle a real book. She owned a complete set of the first edition, probably a gift from her father, an avid novel-reader, or perhaps a present from her mother, who also knew *Grandison* inside out.[20] On the title-page of each of the seven volumes 'Jane' is written in the top left-hand corner, 'Austen' in the top right, in a neat and somewhat laboriously formed copperplate, obviously the writing of a child. These signatures are undated. But it is reasonable to suppose that they were inscribed well before 1790.[21] By that time she was sufficiently in possession of the novel and sufficiently confident to be poking fun at it in the early satires.

Where does all this leave the story of Anna's authorship? Her role must have been much more modest; and, once again, the manuscript can help us towards a precise answer. On the title-page and other early pages there are pencil scribblings in a childish hand, and other childish alterations in ink. It is quite possible that during Anna's later visits to Steventon, between 1796 and 1800, Jane Austen was working intermittently on 'Grandison', revising and continuing the early pages, with the young niece at her elbow, offering suggestions and even being allowed, as a special privilege, to write on the manuscript itself— inserting a word or two here and there, changing a phrase, bringing a character on stage. That, almost certainly, was the extent of Anna's contribution; and if we grace it with the name of collaboration, that was the sum of it.

No one could blame Anna for remembering, later in life, her slight contribution as much more. No doubt Jane Austen encouraged the little girl to imagine that she had really supplied the ideas for the play and that Aunt Jane had simply written them down! Perhaps, too, Anna did provide an Act Six a few years later, just as she added further pages to the manuscript of one of her aunt's childhood stories.[22] With such an aunt, which one of us would not be guilty of some slight and flattering misrecollection! Nor can one blame her daughter and later generations for accepting the story at face value. Anna's memory was usually detailed and accurate and she was one of the principal sources for her brother's *Memoir*.[23] She was commonly regarded in the family as Jane Austen's literary heir and the inheritor, in a lesser way, of her literary talents. As Francis Austen has suggested to me, it may well be that it was Anna's 'private and intrinsic regard for this intimate memento of her aunt that unwittingly gave rise to the "myth" developed in succeeding generations'.[24] In these circumstances, it is easy to see how the tradition of Anna's authorship came into being, how it was sustained, and how, as a consequence, 'Grandison' now comes to be added to the Jane Austen canon only at this late date.

*

Coming to 'Grandison' from the novels, as most people will do, the reader faces the essential difference between Jane Austen's public writing and the private work. The novels belong to one world, 'Grandison' to another: not the world of the reviewers and public judgement but the close and intimate circle of the Austens and their friends. Steventon Rectory was the home of a highly gifted and literate family. Much of the entertainment was of their own making. Little stories and essays circulated round the family; they read aloud in the family circle; acted their own simple charades and dramatic sketches and put on full-scale plays, sometimes with verse-Prologues and Epilogues provided by James. This *family* aspect is very evident in 'Grandison'. It part-lampoons, part-imitates a favourite family novel and carries a substratum of Austen jokes and references. It was a play for the family to perform. The stage directions are working directions, telling the actors what to do and where to go and leaving little to chance or to the players' uncertainty. So if we set up 'Grandison' for performance in our mind's eye, as many readers will do, we should view it with generosity and good humour, just as the family party would have done in 1800, delighted to see their friends and relations stumbling through their half-learnt lines, perhaps taking parts that touched amusingly or embarrassingly upon themselves in real life—a game that Jane Austen played seriously in *Mansfield Park* with the rehearsals for *Lovers' Vows*.

No one should be surprised, then, to find 'Grandison' a mixed bag. Alongside the few moments of high farce and comic melodrama, and the flashes of wit and the lines broadly hammable, there are *longueurs*, snatches of dialogue and stretches of action that lead nowhere. This is exactly what one would expect to find in a piece of home-theatricals which provided parts for the children as well as for the grown-ups, and which allowed the youngsters a line or two or the chance to make a brief appearance on-stage to hand round the tea-cups!

Although this is Jane Austen's only play, she was by no means ignorant of the dramatist's craft or of the capacities and incapacities of an amateur cast. Among the Austens there was a long tradition of family theatricals and their 'theatrical troop',[25] as it was known, attempted some ambitious plays. Visitors were pressed into service; indeed, were not given house-room unless they undertook to join in! Mrs Austen would declare that they had no room 'for any idle young people'.[26] As far back as 1784, when Jane Austen was nine, they had put on Sheridan's *The Rivals* and we have details of a number of later productions.[27] In summer, the Rector's barn was fitted up as a little theatre and at Christmas they either played there or in the Rectory dining-room. The great comic moment in *Mansfield Park*—when Sir Thomas Bertram returns unexpectedly to find his study in disorder and the Hon. Mr Yates next door in the billiard-room spouting his lines as 'the impassioned Baron Wildenhaim' may have sprung from a similar incident in the home of the Revd. George Austen. And this is the kind of episode that may also stand behind the first scene of 'Grandison', where Mr Reeves congratulates himself on having prevented the womenfolk from invading his study with their 'Dresses & Band boxes'. Anna Austen remembered her grandfather's study as just such a preserve: 'his own exclusive property, safe from the bustle of all household cares'.[28]

For Jane Austen, the earliest outcome of the family theatricals were her own little comedies, joke-playlets, of which only three have survived.[29] These were probably written between 1787 and 1790. Two of the three she copied into the juvenilia notebook *Volume the First*: 'The Visit: A Comedy in 2 Acts', five pages long; and 'The Mystery', which lives up to its title by scattering hints and unfinished statements and ends by explaining nothing. In *Volume the Second*, there is a three-page trifle, 'The First Act of a Comedy', a fantasy piece, much of it written in rhyme, including a father and daughter named Popgun and Pistoletta. These pieces were written to entertain the family, to be read aloud rather than acted. 'The Mystery' seems to have been modelled on Act Two, Scene One, of Sheridan's *The Critic*. Although the exact target of the other two playlets is uncertain, they are aimed at the minor drama of the period, the plays that the Austens read together and performed.

In the *Memoir*, where he reprinted 'The Mystery', James Edward Austen-Leigh commented that this was 'a specimen of the kind of transitory amusement which Jane was continually supplying to the family party'.[30] 'Grandison' may have begun in the same way, as nothing more than a five-minute squib. The first ten pages of the manuscript are much earlier than the rest, with the title-page carefully laid-out, in the style of a formal cast-list, exactly as if this was the preliminary to a full-scale play. This form of mock-opening we also see in 'The Mystery' and 'The First Act of a Comedy'; and, at the time, Jane Austen may have had little idea how the joke was going to be developed. She had not decided how many acts there were to be, nor the actual cast. The cast-list she wrote down includes the names of characters who make no appearance in the play; while characters who do appear are missing from it. This suggests that to begin with Jane Austen was merely toying with the idea of a *Grandison* play, that she opened it, with mock-formality, as a brief joke, tried it out for the space of a first act and then put the manuscript to one side.

It is difficult to say exactly when this happened. But there is an important clue in the fact that the comedy of the first act is treated realistically, whereas, for example, the *Grandison* satire in 'Love and Friendship', which is dated June 1790, runs to the kind of extravagant burlesque and fantasy that we find in the early juvenilia. The shift towards more realistic satire is marked in the 'Collection of Letters' (also in *Volume the Second*), which has been assigned to 1791-2; and it is on this comparative evidence that we can give an approximate dating, in the same period, for the opening of 'Grandison'.

We have to imagine what happened next: that Jane Austen laid aside the unpromising first act and busied herself with other more rewarding writing—the later juvenilia, collected in the manuscript notebooks; *Lady Susan*, a short novel-in-letters, probably written about 1793-4; and, in turn, the original versions of the three early novels, the last of which, *Northanger Abbey*, was finished in 1799. 'Grandison' was probably taken up again and continued, about that time, when someone in the family, perhaps Anna, suggested that Aunt Jane might provide them with a performable play. In this way, 'Grandison' may have been completed, the last pages written in haste as everyone waited for the script to be finished so that rehearsals could begin. At this final stage, Anna would have enjoyed a privileged place, hoping for a part, offering suggestions and delighted to be able to join with her in writing on the manuscript itself. We cannot put precise dates to this sequence of events. But Act Two is on paper watermarked 1799; and there is a reference within the play which points to the summer or christmas of 1800 as the likely date.

This reference comes in Act Three, where Charlotte offers to play Harriet's favourite tune, 'Laure & Lenze'. There is no record of any song or musical piece with exactly this title. But in May 1800 there was the first performance of *Laura and Lenza*, announced as 'a Grand Fairy Ballet' in two acts, the music by Cesare Bossi. It was staged in London at the King's Opera House in the Haymarket and given sixteen performances during the season which ended on 2 August that year. Possibly Jane Austen or Cassandra or others of the family had seen the ballet. Both sisters were keen theatre-goers and we know from her letters that Jane Austen had an appreciative eye for the absurdities of such entertainments,[31] which were usually rather undistinguished programme-fillers, played as entr'actes or after the main work. And the 'tune' of *Laura and Lenza*, its 'air', could have been known to the Steventon audience through a piano arrangement. Such arrangements were undemanding versions for amateurs to play at home and usually appeared within a few weeks of the first night.[32] As we meet it in 'Grandison', the mention of 'Laure & Lenze' sounds a trifle forced; the dialogue at this point is very wooden; and it seems that Jane Austen was bringing in a current allusion for everyone to applaud for its immediacy and its blatant anachronism, and perhaps also for some private joke. Had someone in the family driven everyone to distraction by strumming it again and again? Or was it the favourite of whoever played Harriet?

In the summer of 1801, Mr Austen resigned his parish duties to James and left Steventon with his wife and two daughters to live in Bath. So the Steventon performance, if it ever did take place, is likely to have been within the space of those last two years.[33]

We can do little more than conjecture about the genesis and completion of 'Grandison'. None the less, even this sketchy account makes it clear that there is no point in making any comparison between the play and the novels, even though the three early novels were written during the same period, prior to 1800.[34] The qualities we find in the novels—the comedy and wit, the vitality and depth of characterization, the elegance and economy of design—are the achievements of high art and they stem from a process of writing and rewriting which lasted many years. The final version of *Sense and Sensibility* was not completed until 1810, of *Pride and Prejudice* until 1812, while *Northanger Abbey* was being finally revised as late as 1816. 'Grandison's' history is entirely different. Begun early, it was finished hurriedly without any attempt to improve the first section or to carry out any methodical revision of the play as a whole.

From a purely literary standpoint, 'Grandison' is indeed no more than a piece of 'transitory amusement' and no one will be surprised to find it at a far remove from the great Jane Austen.

*

The most obvious stumbling-block for the modern reader is that the comedy of 'Grandison' is largely the comedy of allusion. The amusement lies in seeing the way in which the characters, situations, and even the language of the novel are imitated, echoed, and rearranged. Clearly, Jane Austen enjoyed herself in devising a style of allusive counterpoint that calls for nothing less than a verbatim knowledge of *Grandison*—and in her audience at Steventon she could confidently assume this. It was one of the great novels of the age, a particular favourite with the Austens; and by 1800 the family had already met a succession of *Grandison* jokes in the juvenilia and the early novels. Most recently, *Grandison* had featured in *Northanger Abbey*, completed only the year before, where it is named as Mrs Morland's favourite reading, is dismissed by Isabella Thorpe as 'an amazing horrid book', and abandoned by her friend, Miss Andrews, before she reached the end of even the first volume! In the twentieth century, it has fared even worse. It languishes as a great classic unread. If students of English literature take up any Richardson at all, it will be one of the earlier novels, *Pamela* or *Clarissa*. Few turn to *Grandison*, with its chilling reputation for long-windedness and tedium, and its unstomachably perfect hero.

Of course, there are other views. Blake came to know the novel intimately. Engraving a set of illustrations for an edition of *Grandison*, he declared to a friend, 'Richardson has won my heart.' Hazlitt regarded it, alongside *Don Quixote*, as *the* great European novel. George Eliot was an intolerant admirer: 'Like

Sir Charles Grandison? I should be sorry to be the heathen that did not like that book.'[35] But if one critic has put his finger upon the weaknesses and greatness of *Grandison*, it is Leslie Stephen: 'The virtuous characters give and receive an amount of eulogy enough to turn the strongest stomachs.' Yet he also points to the novel's imaginative force: 'Any one who will get through the initial difficulties and read himself fairly into the story . . . will end by acknowledging the author's power . . . The intensity of Richardson's belief in the creatures of his own imagination is one main secret of the fascination which can still exist.'[36]

What was true for Leslie Stephen at the end of the nineteenth century was certainly true for readers a hundred years earlier. *Grandison* exerted an evident 'fascination' for the young Jane Austen. And if this Introduction seems to concentrate on the satirizible aspects of the novel, we should remind ourselves that 'Grandison' is as much a tribute as a skit. In 1814, when she was corresponding with Anna about 'Which is the Heroine?', Jane Austen explained that she allowed a certain 'Latitude' to 'desultory novels', '& think Nature and Spirit cover many sins of a wandering story'. Put to that test, the desultoriness of *Grandison* is far outweighed by its 'Nature' and 'Spirit', what we would today describe as its truth to human nature and its liveliness of style and wit.

In the notes that follow the play, I have tried to meet the question of unfamiliarity by referring to the specific details of *Grandison* that Jane Austen works into the text. At best, however, this kind of footnoting can only provide a fragmentary impression of the ways in which Jane Austen drew upon the novel. So, in this later part of the Introduction, it may be useful, first to outline the *Grandison* story, then to indicate the novel's general character, and, finally, to discuss Jane Austen's dramatization.

The plot of Grandison draws upon some of the standard situations and complications of eighteenth-century drama and fiction, many of them borrowed from Restoration comedy. Harriet Byron, an attractive and marriageable heroine, comes to London at the age of twenty to be launched in society. At home, in Northamptonshire, she was surrounded by admirers; and in London she finds many more. After a masquerade ball, she is abducted by the most persistent of them, Sir Hargrave Pollexfen. He tries to bully her through a marriage ceremony at Paddington. Failing in that, he sweeps her off towards his cottage in Windsor Forest. *En route* Harriet is saved in true heroic style by Grandison. It is a meeting of noble natures: she duly falls in love with him and he with her. But there is a complication—his engagement to an Italian noblewoman, Clementina della Poretta. His dilemma is to be in love with two women at the same time. The centre of the novel, from Volume Three to Volume Six, is occupied with the negotiation of these delicate issues. But all ends happily, in England at least. Clementina releases Grandison; the shadow of a mixed, Catholic marriage is dispelled (not the marriage for a gentleman of such sound English stock); and, to everyone's satisfaction, the hero and heroine are united.

Grandison is a novel in letters, the form which Jane Austen herself used for the short novel *Lady Susan*, probably written in 1793–4, and for the original version of *Sense and Sensibility*, written a year or so later. It was Richardson's favourite method and he handles it so skilfully and freely that there is no loss of dramatic impact in the narration of the events and no muffling of the dialogue. Quite often, we forget that we are reading an epistolary novel. Occasionally, the dialogue is presented exactly as in a play-script, a device which may have suggested the idea of a *Grandison* play to Jane Austen. She would have been impressed, too, by the two main women characters, Harriet Byron and Charlotte Grandison, the hero's younger sister. Most of the correspondence is between women; and for much of the novel, the woman's account is the prevailing point of view. This is a remarkable feat of 'feminine' style and 'feminine' imaginative understanding. It is unparalleled in eighteenth-century fiction, even by women writers themselves. Amongst the hordes of lady novelists, not excluding Fanny Burney, there is no one who even approaches Richardson in forming a credible female consciousness, a character with self-awareness and an experiencing mind. To match the powerful reality of Charlotte Grandison, the novel's undisputed triumph, we have to look back to Shakespeare or forward to Jane Austen herself, to the vitality and rebelliousness of Marianne Dashwood and the sparkling aggressiveness of Elizabeth Bennet.

Grandison is an extensive and leisurely moral comedy-of-manners, often very amusing, well-observed, and delivered with wit and style. Its best passages remind us of Jane Austen. They have, as it were, the character of proto-Austen, but without the organization and economy of her art. What sinks the novel, however, is its hero. Unlike Charlotte, a genuine dramatic creation, with a life of her own, Grandison is drawn to an unpromising formula. According to Richardson, he was to be a type of hero entirely new to English fiction: 'a Man of TRUE HONOUR . . . A Man of Religion and Virtue; of Liveliness and Spirit; accomplished and agreeable; happy in himself, and a Blessing to others.'[37] He was designed to embody—morally, materially, and spiritually—all that is signalled in his *Grand*-sounding name. He was to be an anti-Tom Jones: quite the opposite of a laughable, lovable, low-life rascal. He was a hero *sans héroïques*: cast not in the ancient heroic mould, with feats of arms and promiscuous gallantry, but a model brand-new: a paragon of gentle gentlemanliness, of English virtues and Christian benevolence, Chaucer's 'verray parfit gentil knight' translated into the mid-Augustan chivalry of domestic honour, social cultivation, and the errantry of good works. So he stands at the centre of the novel, a universal 'Blessing', attended by a circle of admiring men and adoring females (a devitalized Harriet among them, now a woman in tow), all rejoicing in his presence!

Much of the novel's length is accounted for by Richardson's elaborate portrayal of Grandison's benevolent activities and his heart-and-conscience-searching over Clementina. Sir Walter Scott put Richardson's presentation of Clementina on a level with *Clarissa*; here, he said, were 'the passages of deep pathos on which his claim to immortality must finally rest.'[38] Pathos there may be. But whatever life there is in the Italian episodes is remote from the kind of vitality that surrounds Charlotte Grandison; and remote, too, from the Jane Austen-like satire that flavours the early letters of Harriet Byron. Those parts of the novel are entertaining and attached to characters for whom we feel something. What makes the Italian affairs so inert is not Clementina but a hero so lacking in human interest; and it is easy to see what sections of the novel Henry Austen had in mind when he spoke of Richardson's 'prolix style and tedious narrative'.

*

The essence of the joke in Jane Austen's 'Sir Charles Grandison' is the reduction of a mammoth novel to a miniature play. It is a *reductio ad absurdum*, a pin-prick to deflate *Grandison's* epic proportions and the elaboration and leisureliness of its procedure. To unite the hero and heroine in six long volumes, with yet another volume on top! Jane Austen's retort is to bring about the marriage in the space of five short acts, a comedy of abridgement.

In fact, the play may have begun precisely as an 'abridgement' joke, in parallel with 'The History of England'. The 'History' is a comic satire on Goldsmith's *Abridgement* (1774) of his own *History of England* (1764). The opening pages of 'Grandison' could well have been written about the same time and to the same pattern, since abridgements of *Grandison* also abounded.[39] Like the abridgements of English history, they too were designed for children, suitably potted and bowdlerized. Jane Austen's 'History' plays a double trick in being highly potted but quite unbowdlerized! She makes a point of attending to the scandals of our kings and queens. The same spirit of fun roams freely in 'Grandison'. The schoolroom versions were notably reticent in retailing the events at Paddington, where the threat of rape hangs heavy in the air. Jane Austen makes this the high point of her comic melodrama. Far from closing her eyes to the strain of erotic titillation in Richardson, Jane Austen laughs it off the stage.

The comedy of abridgement and the comedy of allusion are both neatly joined in the play's subtitle. 'The happy man' is a key phrase of the novel. He is, naturally, the happily *married* man or the man about to be married, in line with those other popular sayings, also in *Grandison*, the 'happy day', 'the happy pair'. 'The happy man' of *Grandison* is of course the hero himself, to whom this phrase and other 'happy' variants are attached with some frequency. They are also attached, less prominently to other characters, to such an extent that the happy marriage idea echoes and re-echoes through the novel rather insistently. Richardson designed *Grandison* as a kind of conduct-book, a didactic entertainment, from which young people could take an enjoyable and instructive lesson in manners, in behaviour correct for polite society. The exemplary happy marriage is part of this message. Jane Austen's playful use of the phrase at the head of 'Grandison' is not to question the spirit of the message but to mimic the unsubtle way in which Richardson drums it out. Probably it was one of the stock *Grandison* jokes amongst the Austens; and, for them, the subtitle would be a clear indication of the satire to come.

'Grandison' opens with a scene wholly of Jane Austen's

devising and with no direct source in the novel. But the Steventon audience would know exactly where they were in the story. The entry of Mrs Reeves and the Milliner and the topic of dresses are clearly to do with Harriet's fateful attendance at the masquerade ball. We have to be cautious about ascribing a deep satirical purpose to this scene. Its deficiencies as a piece of dramatic writing are obvious enough and this could be put down to the author's inexperience. On the other hand, the very commonplaceness and banality of the dialogue could be part of the joke. *Grandison's* vast proportions and the minute detail in which Richardson works, have the effect of dignifying, sometimes comically over-dignifying, domestic scenes of this kind. Here, Jane Austen seems to be saying, instead of the literary magnification of Richardson, is the real-life smallness and triviality of the woman's world. It may be that this idea was partly suggested to her by a lively passage in Volume Six (Letter 47), where Charlotte holds forth on female egocentricity and self-importance: 'We women are sad creatures for delaying things to the last moment. We hurry the men: We hurry our work-women, milaners, mantuamakers, friends, allies, confederates, and ourselves . . . And why should not we women, after all, contrive to make hurry-skurries . . . and make the world think our affairs a great part of the business of it, and that nothing can be done without us?'

This touches on the battle-of-the-sexes, a theme that Richardson voices wittily and aggressively through Charlotte and which Jane Austen immediately continues here in the mutterings of Mr Reeves about the goings-on of the womenfolk and their invading 'Dresses & Band boxes'. With Mr Reeves, Jane Austen makes an amusing reversal. Richardson's Mr Reeves is comically meek and mild, quite incapable of the 'Raillery' which Harriet fears from him (in the novel, it is Mr

Selby's raillery she has to suffer) and altogether without the 'spirit' with which he credits himself.

Jane Austen bases Scene Three—where Mr Reeves organizes the search for Harriet, after the ball—upon a letter from him to Mr Selby, Harriet's guardian in Northamptonshire, reporting her disappearance and the state of the household. There seems no obvious satirical point to the scene. Probably it was there to help the story along and provide some small servants' parts for the children. The sole point of literary interest is to see how Jane Austen has translated the breathless style of Richardson's letter into Mr Reeves's agitation on stage.

The play comes to life in Act Two, a burlesque version of the attempted marriage. To construct this, Jane Austen drew upon a sequence of letters in Volume One, keeping to the same characters and following much of the circumstance and verbal detail. The essential change is not the dramatization—for the pattern of Richardson's dialogue and the style of the action are already highly dramatic, not to say melodramatic—but in the shift of tone. And to turn this part of the novel into broad farce, as Jane Austen does, required only the slightest tilt.

Up to this point in *Grandison*, Richardson had succeeded in making Pollexfen a reasonably credible figure, an Augustan-Restoration literary villain—a rakish, boorish man about town, a self-conceited seducer, who assumes that Harriet will be bowled over by his striking looks, his money, his title, his arrogance, and his smooth talk. Richardson makes a fine scene of his earlier collision with Harriet. She sees him for what he is— vain, bumptious, and offensive—and tells him 'the simplest truth', that he does not 'hit' her 'fancy' (Volume One, Letter 17). Jane Austen learnt a great deal from this side of Richardson. But when it came to the drama of action, Richardson was inept; and the Paddington events are, just as Jane Austen presents them, knockabout farce. Pollexfen pops in and out of the room in a series of inexplicable entrances and exits, the stage villain *par excellence*.

Pollexfen has become a strutting, moustache-twirling, eighteenth-century Sir Jasper, throwing out dark and heavy hints—what will happen to his victim if she refuses marriage, her power to provoke him, his own desperation, leading to her 'ruin'. Rape is never spoken but its anticipation is heavy in the air. Richardson's imaginative energies are engaged in forming the image of a man aroused, and his arousing and temptingly innocent victim. The formula sounds promising. In *Clarissa*, Richardson had already succeeded in creating a reality in which the sense of evil and danger is genuinely disturbing. But in *Grandison* such a level of human drama is missing. What we get instead is ridiculous titillation and coarse suggestiveness. This was material ready-made for a literary joke. Those of the family who already knew *Northanger Abbey* would have recognized Pollexfen in the ancestry of those wicked baronets who—as Mrs Morland might have warned her daughter—'delight in forcing young ladies away to some remote farm-house'.[40]

There is a ludicrous moment in Volume One when Harriet tries to escape, struggles in the doorway, and has her stomach squeezed—a squeezing which inspires some of the classic lines in the repertoire of expiring heroines: 'So, so, you have killed me, I hope—Well, now I hope, now I hope, you are satisfied' (Letter 31). Again, true to her heroine role, Harriet also suffers a succession of fainting-fits, from which, however, she is sometimes mercifully preserved by the onset of a 'frenzy'. For, as she explains, 'I was in a perfect frenzy: But it was not an unhappy frenzy; since in all probability, it kept me from falling into fits; and fits, the villain had said, should not save me' (Letter 31).

Who could resist humour so beautifully unconscious? Or targets so readily available? Jane Austen's burlesque in Act Two is deadly accurate and shows up the weakest and most vulnerable side of Richardson—his ineptness in the handling of action, his streak of prurience, and the doggedness with which he pursues certain topics throughout the length of the novel. An instance of this are the 'fits' and 'faints' suffered by Harriet (discussed more fully in the notes on p. 137). Between them, Harriet and Clementina run through the whole gamut of female nervous and hysterical conditions. It was a subject that fascinated Richardson and upon which he was remarkably well informed, as the publisher of two medical works in this very area. In *Grandison*, this obsessive expertise is not worn lightly; and it is pretty certain that such 'fits', 'faints', and other feminine complaints provided another standing joke for the play's audience at Steventon.

Acts Three to Five move through *Grandison* swiftly and glancingly. There is no attempt to follow its plot systematically. What we have is a sequence of loosely connected scenes, from the morning after Harriet's abduction until the arrival of the guests for her wedding. Throughout, the location is Colnebrook, the country house to which Grandison brings Harriet following her rescue. There is no return to the boisterousness of Act Two. From here onwards 'Grandison' is an imitative pastiche of the drawing-room comedy-of-manners. The dialogue is derived largely from the elaborately polite, often stilted form of conversation that goes on in the Grandison family circle. Vestigial as they are, the main characters—Harriet, Charlotte, and Grandison himself—are recognizably taken from their originals in the novel. Harriet is a rather colourless admiring female—just as she becomes, disappointingly, in *Grandison*, her liveliness and independence lost once she has been saved by the hero. Charlotte is the rebel, the mischief-maker, sharp and outspoken, the cheeky younger sister, the only one who has enough spirit to say boo to Grandison. Jane Austen's joke here is to vulgarize her slightly, making her sound like another Isabella Thorpe. Grandison is the man of high honour, of mysterious enterprises, a covert do-gooder (eulogized by Charlotte in Act Three, Scene One), brought down to earth only when he has to deal with his sister's bad manners.

Occasionally, Grandison is enlivened with some quite un-Richardsonian humour—such as the moment in Act Four, when his elder sister is late for tea and the hero cracks what is for him a daring joke: 'How long Caroline has been gone! I hope no more Sir Hargrave Pollexfens have run away with her & Emily.' 'Pictures of perfection', Jane Austen told one of her nieces, 'make me sick & wicked'.[41] The satire in 'Grandison' is not of that order. But, taken as a whole, the play is a shrewd and amusing swipe at the character of Richardson's 'happy man'.

Finally, it is worth noting one particular area in which Jane Austen departs from the *Grandison* story. I have already mentioned her creation of the opening scene. Another such creation is Act Five, Scene One, the light comedy of Mr Selby's discouraging response to Grandison's application for Harriet's hand in marriage. In the novel, Grandison has to go to Selby House in Northamptonshire and it is a matter not of Mr Selby's consent but the approval of Harriet's closest relatives; while the marriage-terms are nothing to do with Mr Selby but are in the hands of her godfather, Mr Deane. Jane Austen makes Harriet eighteen instead of twenty. The further change is Grandison's reference here to the possibility of a double-marriage—his own and that of his sister and Lord G. In the novel, this is an arrangement that Charlotte would have liked; but it happens that she marries first, on 11 April, Harriet on 15 November. There is no obvious point of satire in these changes and my own guess is that Jane Austen introduced them in order to connect 'Grandison' with a recent or forthcoming marriage in the family, or in one of the families of the neighbourhood. There is no direct evidence for this. But throughout the juvenilia literary allusions are intermingled with references to the Austen family and their friends.[42] In 'The Three Sisters', for example, in *Volume the First*, Mary Stanhope insists that her husband-to-be shall build her 'a Theatre to act Plays in. The first Play we have shall be *Which is the Man*, and I will do Lady Bell Bloomer.' Mrs Cowley's *Which is the Man* was the Christmas play at Steventon in 1787. Writing now for a later generation, Jane Austen would have been no less keen that 'Grandison' should continue this tradition of family allusion.

*

Much more can be said about the interconnections between 'Grandison' and Richardson's novel; and no doubt later commentators and critics will take this exploration further. What I have wanted to do here is to indicate the obvious aspects of the relationship, sufficiently to enable the reader to grasp the method and working of Jane Austen's allusive comedy. On the literary front, the satire is easily accessible. However, what is lost to us is 'Grandison's' attachment to the Austen family. In the course of the Introduction, I have been able to point to several instances where it is reasonable to suppose that family jokes are being sounded. But this is guesswork; and in the absence of any contemporary evidence, guesswork it must remain. I regret this, since my personal impression is that the play's allusiveness is as much domestic as literary and that the Rectory audience would be as much entertained and flattered by the family aspect of 'Grandison' as by its literary satire.

The importance of 'Grandison' remains debatable. The news of its discovery brought the comment that this was a great fuss about very little and that trivia of this kind should be left to slumber in decent obscurity. The same issue arose a century ago, when the first edition of the *Memoir* was so warmly received that a second edition was called for almost at once. Correspondents urged James Edward Austen-Leigh to enlarge the book with examples of Jane Austen's childhood writing and extracts from the unpublished manuscripts. This he did, though not without opposition from the family: 'the vexed question between the Austens and the Public',[43] as his sister Caroline described the issue, was touched upon once again. Anna had no objection to the inclusion of the juvenilia: 'What I should deprecate is publishing any of the "Betweenities" when the nonsense was passing away, and before her wonderful talent had found its proper channel.'[44] 'Grandison' is, of course, a very private betweenity, and, on this judgement, should never see the light of day.

When it comes to argument, there is little to say. Beside the novels, 'Grandison' is indeed no more than a trifle. It adds nothing to the great works, to the Jane Austen the world loves and enjoys. Students have a special stake and will value 'Grandison' as an historical–biographical document and for the light it throws upon her reading of Richardson. For my own part, I can only echo the correspondent who urged James Edward Austen-Leigh to enlarge the *Memoir*, insisting that 'Every line from the pen of Jane Austen is precious'.[45]

NOTES

1. James Edward Austen-Leigh, *Memoir of Jane Austen*, second edition (1871), ed. R. W. Chapman (1926), p. 89.

2. Ibid.

3. p. 240. I have not come across the original of Fanny Lefroy's statement. She did not take the information from the 'Recollections of Jane Austen' listed in the note by Louie Lefroy. These run to fourteen pages and were lot 269 in the same sale as the manuscript of 'Grandison'. Nor is it contained in the transcripts of two

documents given to me by Miss Helen Lefroy: a 'Memoranda' by Anna Austen, copied in September 1872 by her daughter Louis Langlois Lefroy (Mrs Bellas); a second 'Memoranda' by Anna Austen, 'Chiefly copied from an older book, partly from pocket books, letters etc.'

4. W. and R. A. Austen-Leigh, *Jane Austen: Her Life and Letters* (1913), p. 73.

5. Quoted in *Life and Letters*, p. 15.

6. For example, see 'Evelyn', *Volume the Third*, in which Sir Charles Grandison is mentioned and where the hero, Mr Gower, is Grandisonian in his social aplomb and perfections, and is addressed, just as Grandison is in the novel, as 'best of men'; also 'Jack & Alice', *Volume the First*, where Grandison is again mentioned and where Charles Adams is another Grandisonian hero; also 'Love and Friendship', *Volume the Second*, where Laura's perfections seem to be a dig at the perfections of Harriet Byron; and where the particularity and prolixity of detail in Letter the 5th ridicule these aspects of Richardson's style.

7. Hill, pp. 239–40.

8. R. W. Chapman ed., *Jane Austen's Letters*, second edition (1952), Letters 95, 98, 100, 101, 107.

9. This manuscript was sold at Sotheby's, 13 December 1977, Lot 266. One page is reproduced in the catalogue.

10. An attribution proposed by R. Brimley Johnson, *Jane Austen* (1930), p. 224, and enlarged upon by David Gilson, 'Anna Lefroy and "Mary Hamilton"', *The Warden's meeting: a tribute to John Sparrow* (1977), pp. 43–6.

11. Of course, Dr Chapman knew the book by Constance Hill. In *Jane Austen: Facts and Problems* (1948), he calls it 'a pleasing account of the family and its environment derived from family papers and traditions' (p. 170). He also gave it an entry (no. 111) in *Jane Austen: A Critical Bibliography* (1953). But how well did he know it? It is just possible that he may have missed Fanny Lefroy's statement.

I suggest this because the entry in the *Critical Bibliography* pays tribute to the book's charm but gives no indication that Hill is a major biographical source and contains information available nowhere else in Jane Austen literature.

Chapman also makes some curious errors. In the *Critical Bibliography* he refers to a guess by R. Brimley Johnson, in 1930, that the *Temple Bar* article (cited here in note 20) was written by Fanny Lefroy. But he ignores the reference in Hill (p. 234), which states that the article was indeed by her. And in his edition of the *Letters* (p. 406), Chapman describes as 'Unpublished' a letter from Jane Austen to Anna which is printed in Hill complete (pp. 195-6).

12. p. 113.

13. Private communication.

14. B. C. Southam, *Jane Austen's Literary Manuscripts* (1964), p. 10, n. 3.

15. Sotheby's Catalogue of Sale for 13 December 1977, Lot 265.

16. See Introduction, pp. 13-14.

17. *Memoir*, ed. Chapman, p. 89. The 'cedar parlour' is Harriet's favourite room in Selby House. There is an error of recollection: there was no wedding-day of Lady L. to remember; she is already married when the novel opens.

18. Elizabeth Jenkins, *Jane Austen* (1938), p. 34.

19. Written December 1817 and printed at the head of *Northanger Abbey and Persuasion* (1817).

20. Fanny Lefroy contributed an article 'Is it Just?' to the *Temple Bar* magazine for February 1883, vol. 67, in which she quotes from one of Mrs Austen's letters to Anna: 'These are the days of what Mr Selby would have called 'hugger-mugger weddings, only fit for doubtful happiness'' . . .'.

21. For these details I am obliged to David Gilson and to his article 'Jane Austen's Books', *The Book Collector* (Spring 1974), pp. 27-39; and to Marquess Conyngham, the present owner of Jane Austen's set of *Grandison*.

22. This was to 'Evelyn' in *Volume the Third*. Three sheets were inserted loosely at the end of the notebook. This must have been after November 1814, the year of Anne's marriage, as the addition is signed J. A. E. L., the initials of her married name. For a fuller discussion, see B. C. Southam, 'Interpolations to Jane Austen's "Volume the Third" ', *Notes and Queries* (May 1962), pp. 185-7.

23. James Edward Austen-Leigh pays ample tribute in the *Memoir* itself and there is an impressive confirmation from his daughter, Mary Augusta Austen-Leigh, in *Personal Aspects of Jane Austen* (1920), p. 4.

24. Private communication.

25. R. A. Austen-Leigh ed., *Austen Papers 1704-1856* (1942), pp. 148-9.

26. *Life and Letters*, pp. 64-5, quotes from the letters of Philadelphia Walter (a daughter of the Revd. George Austen's half-brother) and Eliza de Feuillide (a daughter of George Austen's older sister) on this point.

27. See Southam, *Jane Austen's Literary Manuscripts*, p. 8.

28. Quoted in *Life and Letters*, p. 15.

29. In the 'Dedication' to 'The Visit', Jane Austen writes of this piece as being 'inferior to those celebrated Comedies called "The School for Jealousy" & "The travelled Man".' These titles are otherwise unknown and they must be companion-pieces to the three surviving playlets; and there may well have been others.

30. *Memoir*, p. 44.

31. Unfortunately, we have no letters for this period; there is a gap from 19 June 1799 to 25 October 1800. But we get an insight into the sisters' theatrical interests in Jane Austen's letters to Cassandra of 8 and 25 January 1801 *(Letters*, pp. 107, 118); and in some of the letters surviving from 1813, we can read Jane Austen's views on similar entertainments *(Letters*, pp. 321, 338, 380, 384).

32. The scores in the British Library are undated. The attributed dates are 1803, 1804, 1807, 1808, and 1810. These successive editions lend force to the claim on one title-page that 'Laura and Lenza' was

a 'much admired air'; and Roger Fiske tells me that the music he has for two other of Bossi's ballets is by no means rubbish and well above average for such things.

33. According to the *Life and Letters* (p. 66), the last recorded Steventon performances were in January 1790. But J. H. Hubback (the grandson of Jane Austen's brother Francis) says that the theatricals were resumed in about 1794, soon after Eliza de Feuillide returned to Steventon ('Pen Portraits in Jane Austen's Novels', *Cornhill Magazine* (July 1928), pp. 24–33). Then C. L. Thompson tells us that by 1797, Eliza 'was again helping to organise theatricals at Steventon' (*Jane Austen: A Survey* (1928), p. 18). No source is provided for these details but as the book draws extensively upon Austen family papers, I think it trustworthy; and it would be perfectly in character for Eliza to be taking a leading role. She was a born actress, fun-loving, and extremely vivacious; just the person to revive the theatrical tradition and to take the part of Charlotte Grandison. On 31 December 1797, she married Henry Austen.

34. The original version of *Sense and Sensibility*, about 1795; *Pride and Prejudice*, October 1795 to August 1797; *Northanger Abbey*, 1798 to 1799. These datings are fully discussed in Southam, pp. 52–5.

35. Blake, in a letter to William Hayley, 18 July 1804. George Eliot, in a letter to Bessie Parkes, 30 October 1852.

36. Introduction to *The Works of Samuel Richardson* (1883–4), pp. xxxiv, liv, lv.

37. Preface to *Grandison*.

38. Introduction to *Ballantyne's Novelists' Library*, vol. 1 (1825).

39. Selections, condensations, and abridgements accompanied *Grandison* down the eighteenth century. One popular version, which Jane Austen may have encountered is *The History of Sir Charles Grandison abridged from the works of Samuel Richardson*. It reached a tenth edition by 1798, selling for one shilling. The text is 138 pages, about 25,000 words.

40. *Northanger Abbey*, ch. 2. There are other cross-references in 'Grandison'. Charlotte Grandison is sometimes given the style of

fashionable slang that we hear from Isabella Thorpe. And we are reminded of the lecture Henry Tilney delivers to Catherine Morland on the use and misuse of 'nice' (ch. 14): on p. 23 of 'Grandison' we see 'nice' misused, on p. 44 and 46 we see it properly used, in Tilney's terms, with a precise differentiation of meaning—in the first instance 'choosey', in the second 'particular'.

41. 'pictures of perfection as you know make me sick & wicked'; to Fanny Knight, 23 March 1817, *Letters*, pp. 486–7.

42. Discussed in Southam, pp. 6–8.

43. Quoted by R. W. Chapman, *Facts and Problems*, p. 140.

44. *Facts and Problems*, p. 144, where it is attributed to Anna's half-sister, Caroline Austen. But in the *Critical Bibliography*, p. 33, Chapman attributes 'betweenities' to Anna. As the *Critical Bibliography* was published in 1953, I am assuming this later statement to be correct.

45. Quoted by Mary Augusta Austen-Leigh, 'Jane Austen: A Personal Aspect', *Quarterly Review*, vol. ccxxxii (1919), pp. 301–2.

NOTE ON THE READING TEXT

In the preparation of this text for reading and performance, I have tried to confine editorial changes and additions to a bare minimum, correcting one or two obvious mistakes, regularizing spelling and punctuation, reinstating some lines cancelled by Jane Austen, and providing scene locations wherever these are needed.

The nature and extent of the editing can be judged by comparing this text with the four facsimile pages reproduced in this book.

SIR CHARLES GRANDISON

OR

THE HAPPY MAN

A comedy in Five Acts

BY

JANE AUSTEN

Dramatis Personae

MEN

Sir Charles Grandison

Sir Hargrave Pollexfen

Lord L.

Lord G.

Mr Reeves

Mr Selby

Clergyman

Clergyman's Clerk

Mr Smith

John

Thomas

William

Frederic

Footman

WOMEN

Harriet Byron

Lady Caroline L., elder sister of Sir Charles Grandison

Charlotte Grandison, younger sister of Sir Charles Grandison

Mrs Reeves, cousin of Harriet Byron

Mrs Selby, aunt of Harriet Byron

Lucy Selby ⎫ cousins of
Nancy Selby ⎬ Harriet Byron

Emily Jervois, ward of Sir Charles Grandison

Mrs Awberry

Deborah Awberry

Sally Awberry

Milliner

Sally

Jenny

Bridget

ACT ONE

Scene One

The play begins in the drawing-room of Mr and Mrs Reeves's house in Grosvenor Street, London. It is an afternoon sometime in the early 1750s.

Enter MRS REEVES *and the* MILLINER *at different doors.*

MRS R. So, you have brought the dresses, have you?

MILL. I have brought the young lady's dress; and mistress says you may depend upon having yours this evening.

MRS R. Well, tell her to be sure and bring it. But let us see the dress that is come.

She takes the bandbox out of the MILLINER'S *hands.*

MILL. Have you any other commands, madam?

MRS R. No, you may go. Miss Byron and I will come tomorrow and pay you.

Exit MILLINER.

Come, I will see if she has made it right. Oh! but here is Miss Byron coming. I think it is but fair to let her see it first.

Enter MISS BYRON *with a work-bag on her arm.*

MRS R. Here, my dear, is your dress come. I hope it will fit, for if it does not, she will hardly have time to alter it.

MISS B. We will take it upstairs, if you please, and look at it, for Mr Reeves is coming and we shall have some of his raillery.

Exeunt, in a hurry. Enter MR REEVES.

MR R. So, for once in a way I have got the coast clear of dresses and bandboxes. And I hope my wife and Miss Byron will continue to keep their millinery in their own rooms, or anywhere so as they are not in my way. Why, if I had not had a little spirit the other day, I should have had them in my own study!

Enter SALLY.

SALLY. Do you know where Miss Byron is, sir?

MR R. She is up in her own room, I believe.

SALLY *curtseys and goes off.*

MR R. Sally! Sally!

Re-enter SALLY.

SALLY. Sir?

MR R. Tell Thomas to bring out the bay horse.

SALLY. Yes, sir.

Exit SALLY.

MR R. Well, I must go and get on my boots and by that time the horse will be out.

Scene Two

MR REEVES'S *study early the next morning.*

MR REEVES, *entering in a great hurry at one door, and running out at the other, then calls from behind the scenery.*

MR R. [*off-stage*] John, run all over London and see if you can find the chairmen or chair that took Miss Byron. You know what number it was. Thomas, run for Mr Smith directly.

He comes on-stage again, in great agitation. Enter BRIDGET.

BRID. My mistress is rather better, sir, and begs you will send for Mr Smith.

MR R. I have, I have.

Exit BRIDGET *and* MR REEVES *at different doors.* MR REEVES *calls from behind the scenery.*

MR R. [*off-stage*] William, run to Mr Greville's lodgings and if he is at home—Stop, William! Come in here!

MR REEVES *comes in again, with* WILLIAM. *Takes out his writing-box and writes a note in great haste.*

MR R. Here, William, is a note. Carry it to Mr Greville's.

Exit WILLIAM. *Enter* THOMAS.

THOS. Mr Smith, sir.

MR R. Shew him upstairs to your mistress.

Exit THOMAS. *Enter* JOHN.

JOHN. I cannot find either the chair or the chairmen, sir. And Wilson is not come within, sir.

MR R. Well, she must be carried out into the country, I think. You go to Paddington and tell Thomas to go to Hampstead, and see if you can find her, and I will go to Clapham.

Exeunt.

ACT TWO

Early the same morning in the home of MRS AWBERRY *at Paddington.*

The curtain draws up and discovers MISS BYRON *and* MRS AWBERRY. SIR HARGRAVE POLLEXFEN *is visible to the audience, but not to the ladies, at the side of the stage.*

MRS A. But, my dear young lady, think what a large fortune Sir Hargrave has got; and he intends you nothing but marriage.

MISS B. Oh! Mrs Awberry, do you think I can marry a man whom I always disliked and now hate? Is not this your house? Cannot you favour my escape?

MRS A. My dear madam, that is impossible without detection. You know Sir Hargrave is here and there and everywhere.

MISS B. My dear Mrs Awberry, you shall have all the money in this purse if you will release me.

SIR HARGRAVE *bursts into the room.*

SIR H. Mrs Awberry, I see you are not to be trusted with her, you are so tender-hearted. And you, madam!

He snatches the purse out of her hand and flings it on the ground. He goes to the door and calls.

Mr ——! We are ready.

Enter a CLERGYMAN *and his* CLERK.

SIR H. Miss Awberry! You will be bridesmaid, if you please.

He takes hold of MISS BYRON's *hand. Enter* DEBORAH AWBERRY.

Now, madam, all your purses will not save you.

The CLERGYMAN *takes a book out of his pocket.* MISS BYRON *screams and faints away.* MISS SALLY AWBERRY *runs in.*

DEB. Sally, Sally, bring a glass of water directly!

MRS AWBERRY *takes out her salts and applies them to* MISS BYRON's *nose.*

SIR H. I wish women were not quite so delicate, with all their faints and fits!

MISS BYRON *revives.* MISS SALLY *returns with a glass of water and offers it to* MISS BYRON, *who drinks some.*

MRS A. What a long time you have been, child! If she faints again I shall send your sister.

SAL. [*aside*] I am glad of it.

SIR H. Come, sir, we will try again.

Takes hold of MISS BYRON's *hand.* DEBORAH AWBERRY *goes behind her.*

CLERG. [*reading from a prayer-book*] Dearly beloved—

MISS B. I see no Dearly beloveds here and I will not have any!

MISS BYRON *dashes the prayer-book out of his hand.*

CLERG. [*picking it up again*] Oh! my poor book!

SIR H. Begin again, sir, if you please. You shall be well paid for
your trouble.

CLERG. [*reading again*] Dearly beloved—

MISS BYRON *snatches the book out of his hand and flings it in to the fire,
exclaiming*

MISS B. Burn, quick, quick!

The CLERGYMAN *runs to the fire and cries out.*

CLERG. Oh! Sir Hargrave you must buy me another.

SIR H. I will, sir, and twenty more, if you will do the business. Is
the book burnt?

MRS A. Yes, sir—and we cannot lend you one in its place, for we
have lost the key of the closet where we keep our Prayer-books.

SIR H. Well, sir, I believe we must put it off for the present. And if
we are not married in this house, we shall be in mine, in the
Forest.

CLERG. Then I may go, sir, I suppose. Remember the Prayer-
book.

SIR H. Yes, sir. Good morning.

Exit CLERGYMAN *and his* CLERK.

SIR H. I shall be very much obliged to you, Mrs Awberry, if you
and the young ladies will go out of the room for an instant.
I will see if I cannot reason with this perverse girl.

MRS A. Here, Deb and Sal, come out.

Exeunt MRS AWBERRY *and the* MISSES AWBERRY.

MISS B. Oh! do not leave me alone with him, let me go out too.

She runs to the door. SIR HARGRAVE *follows her. She gets half-way
through the door and he, in shutting it, squeezes her. She screams and faints.
He carries her away in his arms to a chair and rings the bell violently. Enter*
MRS AWBERRY, DEBORAH, AND SALLY.

[43]

SIR H. Bring some water directly.

Both the daughters go out. MISS BYRON *revives and exclaims*

MISS B. So, I hope you have killed me at last.

Re-enter DEBORAH *with the water.* SIR HARGRAVE *takes the glass and gives it to* MISS BYRON.

MISS B. No, I thank you. I do not want anything that can give me life.

SIR H. Well, Miss Awberry, you had better get out the cloak. It is four o'clock and she may as well die in my house as in yours.

MRS A. Shall I order the chariot, sir?

SIR H. If you please, ma'am.

DEBORAH *takes a long cloak out of a closet and attempts to put it round* MISS BYRON. MISS BYRON *struggles.*

SIR H. I will put it on, Miss Awberry, if she will not let you.

He puts it on.

Will you help me lead her downstairs, Miss Awberry?

MISS A. Yes, sir.

They both take hold of MISS BYRON. *Enter* SALLY AWBERRY.

SALLY. Can I be of any service, sir?

SIR H. You may hold the candle.

SALLY *takes the candle. Exeunt.*

ACT THREE

Scene One

Some days later, at Colnebrook, west of London, the home of LORD *and* LADY L. *The scene is a living-room at four in the afternoon.*

Enter MISS GRANDISON *and* MISS BYRON.

MISS B. And where is this brother of yours, to whom I am so much endebted?

MISS G. Safe in St. James's Square, I hope. But why, my dear, will you continue to think yourself endebted to him, when he only did his duty?

MISS B. But what must he have thought of me in such a dress? Oh! these odious masquerades!

MISS G. La! my dear, what does it signify what he thinks? He will understand it all in time. Come, if your stomach pains you, you had better go to bed again.

MISS B. No, it does not pain me at all. But how kind it was in my cousin Reeves to come and see me.

MISS G. Yes, he is a very nice man. I like him very much. He disputes charmingly. I thought he would have got the better of me. Well, but my dear Harriet, you have had a letter today. How does my grandmamma Shirley do? And my uncle and aunt Selby and my cousins Lucy and Nancy?

MISS B. They are all very well. I thank you. And my grandmamma thinks herself under the greatest obligation to Sir Charles for being both her and his Harriet's deliverer. For if he had not rescued me, she would have died of a broken heart.

MISS G. Well, really I am very glad he saved you, for both your sakes.
My brother is a charming man. I always catch him doing some good action. We all wish him to be married but he has no time

[45]

for love. At least, he appears to have none. For he is constantly going about from one place to another. But what for, we cannot tell. And we have such a high respect for him that we never interfere with his affairs. I will return in a minute. I am going to fetch my work bag.

Exit MISS GRANDISON.

MISS B. What an odd brother is this! If he is so fond of them, why should he wish them not to know his affairs?

Re-enter MISS GRANDISON.

MISS G. What is the matter, Harriet? What makes you so dull, child? I shall take care not to leave you by yourself again in a hurry, if, on my return, I am to find these gloomy fits have taken hold of you.

Come, I will play you your favourite tune, 'Laure and Lenze'.

MISS B. I was thinking of Sir Hargrave Pollexfen. But be so good as to play my tune.

MISS G. I will directly.

She goes to the harpsichord and plays. After she has done playing, she comes to MISS BYRON *and says*

Come, it is time for you to go to bed. It is four o'clock and you have been up ever since twelve.

Exeunt.

Scene Two

The Library at Colnebrook, a few minutes later. Curtain draws up and discovers MISS GRANDISON *reading.*

MISS G. Well, I think this book would suit Harriet. But here is our Sir Charles come home, I believe. I will go and see.
Oh! here he is.

Enter SIR CHARLES. *She goes to him. He takes her hand.*

SIR C. No more colds, I hope, my dear Charlotte. But, above all, how does our lovely charge do?

MISS G. Oh! much better. She got up at twelve and I have but just sent her to bed.

SIR C. When do you expect Lord and Lady L.?

MISS G. This evening, about six or seven o'clock.

SIR C. Indeed! I am very glad of it.

Enter JENNY.

JEN. Miss Byron would be glad to speak with you, ma'am.

MISS G. Very well, I will come to her.

SIR C. How is your cold, Jenny?

JEN. Quite well, I thank you, sir.

Curtseys and exit.

MISS G. You will excuse me for a minute, Sir Charles. I must obey my summons.

SIR C. Certainly.

Exit MISS GRANDISON.

Well, I must go and speak to Frederic.

Exit.

Scene Three

Colnebrook, a living-room, two or three hours later, following the arrival of LORD *and* LADY L.

Curtain draws up and discovers LORD *and* LADY L., *and* SIR CHARLES *and* MISS GRANDISON *at tea.*

SIR C. So, my lord, you have heard of our new sister?

LORD L. Yes, Sir Charles, and Miss Grandison, by her description of her, has made me long to see her.

MISS G. [*holding some tea*] Frederic, take this to Sir Charles.

SIR C. I hope you will not be disappointed when you see her—I might say *we*, for I have hardly seen her yet.

MISS G. I hope you do not think me a flatterer, Sir Charles.

SIR C. Certainly not, my dear Charlotte.

LADY L. I assure you, Charlotte can flatter sometimes.

MISS G. Oh! for shame, Caroline, I thought you knew better than to tell tales.
Lord L., will you have any more tea?

LORD L. No, I thank you, Charlotte.

LADY L. But Charlotte, how do we come by our new sister? I have not heard that yet.

MISS G. Well, we will go and take a walk in the garden and talk about it.
Frederic, you may take away.
Come, Caroline, make haste, or the fit will be off.
Gentlemen, will you accompany us?

SIR C. Lord L., will you?

LORD L. Certainly.

SIR C. Yes, we will go, Charlotte.

MISS G. Come, make haste. The fit is almost off.

Exeunt.

ACT FOUR

The scene is Colnebrook, one afternoon a few days later.

Curtain draws up and discovers SIR CHARLES, LORD L., MISS GRANDISON, *and* MISS BYRON.

MISS G. What an impudent fellow Lord G. is to make you wait so, Sir Charles. Oh! he is a poor creature.

SIR C. Have patience, my dear Charlotte. Something has most likely detained him.

MISS G. Indeed, Sir Charles, you are too forgiving. If he were to serve me so, he would not get into favour for some time. What say you, Harriet?

MISS B. Indeed, Miss Grandison, you are too severe. Besides, as Sir Charles says, something may detain him; and it is a different thing making a lady wait on a gentleman.
But here ought to be an end to your severity, for the object of it, I believe, is come. I hear him in the hall.

Enter LORD G.

LORD G. I am afraid I have been making you wait, gentlemen.

MISS G. Well, you need not be afraid any longer, for you most certainly have.

SIR C. Fye Charlotte! I do not think that was the civillest thing in the world to say.

LORD G. I hope I have not offended you, madam.

MISS G. Yes, you have, for making my dear brother wait.

SIR C. I will not be bribed into liking your wit, Charlotte. But where is Caroline all this while?

MISS G. She is gone out in her chariot with Emily. But I wonder, Sir Charles, you did not enquire after your *favourite* sister before.

[49]

LORD L. I am sure, Miss Grandison, you cannot reproach your brother with partiality.

But, Sir Charles, is it not time for us to go out riding? If it is not, I am sure Miss Grandison might have spared her severity on Lord G.

SIR C. I assure you, Lord L., that I had not forgot it. But I think it is too late to go out now. It is three o'clock.

Now, Charlotte, hold your tongue. I am sure some raillery is coming out.

He rings the bell.

MISS G. I will not hold my tongue, Sir Charles.

SIR C. Then, Charlotte, if you speak, do not let us have any severity.

MISS G. Very well, I will be good.

Harriet, what is the matter, child? You look languid. I will ring the bell for some broth for you.

SIR C. Spare yourself that bother, my dear Charlotte, I have just rung it.

Enter FREDERIC.

SIR C. Bring some sandwiches and a basin of broth.

Exit FREDERIC.

MISS G. Harriet, should you like your broth up in your own room better?

MISS B. If you please.

MISS G. Well, we will take it up with us.

Enter FREDERIC *with the sandwiches and the broth. He sets them down upon the table. Exit* FREDERIC. MISS G. *takes the broth.*

MISS G. Come, Harriet.

Exit MISS BYRON *and* MISS GRANDISON. SIR CHARLES *hands round the sandwiches.*

SIR C. How long Caroline has been gone! I hope no more Sir Hargrave Pollexfens have run away with her and Emily.

Enter LADY L., MISS GRANDISON, *and* MISS JERVOIS. LORD L. *goes to meet* LADY L., *takes her hand, and leads her to a sopha.*

MISS G. Lord! what a loving couple they are.

SIR C. Charlotte, hold your tongue.

LORD L. And where have you been to, my dear Caroline?

LADY L. Only shopping. But Charlotte, where is Miss Byron?

MISS G. Very safe in her own room. I always send her away when she gapes.

LADY L. Poor creature! I hope she does not gape too often. But, seriously, Charlotte, is she worse or better?

MISS G. Law! Lady L., you are so afraid I shall not take care of her. Why, she is just as she always is—languid at three o'clock. I believe it is because Lord G. always comes about at that time; and she is so sorry to see her poor Charlotte plagued so!

MISS J. Dear Miss Grandison, who plagues you? I am sure Lord G. does not.

MISS G. Emily, you do not know anything of the matter. You must hold your tongue till it is your turn to be called upon.

MISS J. Well, Miss Grandison, I think it is you who tease him. But he will certainly get the better of you at last. He did it once, you know.

[51]

And I do not know what you mean by its being my turn to be called upon.

MISS G. Why, when it is your turn to be married. But you had better not get on Lord L.'s side; for you will be worsted certainly.

But come, is not it time to dress? [*looks at her watch*] Dear me! it is but four.

LORD L. You need not say 'But', Charlotte, for you know we are to dine at half after four to-day.

MISS G. Indeed, my lord, my lady did not tell me so. Well, I will pardon her this time. Come, then, let us go, if it is time.

Exeunt ladies.

LORD L. What an odd girl is Charlotte. But you must not despair, Lord G. I believe she likes you, though she won't own it. I hope Miss Byron, when she is recovered, will have a little influence over her.

SIR C. Indeed, I hope so too. Miss Byron is a charming young woman and I think, from what I have seen of her, her mind is as complete as her person. She is the happy medium between gravity and over-liveliness. She is lively or grave as the occasion requires.

LORD G. Indeed, she is a delightful young woman and only Miss Grandison can equal her. I do not mean any offence to Lady L.

LORD L. Indeed, my lord, I do not take it as such. Caroline is grave, Charlotte is lively. I am fond of gravity, you most likely of liveliness.

Enter a footman.

FOOT. Dinner is on table, my lord.

LORD L. Very well.

Exit footman. Enter LADY L., MISS GRANDISON, MISS BYRON, *and* MISS JERVOIS.

LORD L. Dinner is upon table, my dear Caroline.

LADY L. Indeed. Come, Harriet and all of you.

Exeunt.

ACT FIVE

Scene One

The library at Colnebrook, an early afternoon some months later.

On stage are SIR CHARLES *and* MR SELBY.

MR S. But, my dear Sir Charles, my niece is but eighteen. I will never allow her to marry till she is twenty-two.

I shall take her back into Northamptonshire if you have done nothing but put such notions into the girl's head. I had no notion of my Harriet's coming to this. And, besides, Sir Charles, I never will allow her to marry you till Lady Clementina della Porretta is married.

SIR C. Mr Selby, that has been my objection for some time to making my proposal to Miss Byron. But yesterday I received some letters from Italy in which they have great hopes of Lady Clementina's being soon persuaded to marry. She wishes me, in the same letter, to set her the example by marrying an English woman. I admire Miss Byron very much, but I will never marry her against your consent. And if you had not told me she was eighteen, I should have thought her quite as much as twenty-two. I do not mean by her looks but by her prudence.

MR S. Upon my word, you are a fine fellow. You have done away with all my objections, and if you can get Harriet's consent, you have mine. I hope she will not be nice, for if she do not get a husband now, she never may, for she has refused all the young gentry of our neighbourhood. As to her fortune, I will tell you plainly she has no more than fourteen-thousand pounds.

SIR C. As to her fortune, it is no object to me. Miss Byron herself is a jewel of inestimable value. Her understanding more than makes up for want of fortune.

And now if we can bring Lord G. and my sister Charlotte together we shall have a double wedding. But I am afraid Charlotte is too lively for matrimony.

MR S. Yes, your sister is a fine girl, only she is too nice about an husband. Adsheart! I hope you won't have such a plague with my Harriet as I had with my Dame Selby.

Well, but it is three o'clock. I will go and break it to her. Sir Charles, you may come and stay at the door till you are admitted, you know.

Exeunt.

Scene Two

The drawing-room at Colnebrook, a few days later.

LADY L., MISS GRANDISON, MISS BYRON, *and* MISS JERVOIS.

MISS G. There is something monstrous frightful, to be sure, my dear Harriet, in marrying a man that one likes.

LADY L. My dear Charlotte, you overfrown Harriet with your raillery. I dare say you will feel the same fright when you marry Lord G.

MISS G. I will tell you what, Lady L. To tell you a secret, I am not likely to marry Lord G., for I want to be married at home and my brother will not consent to it.

MISS J. Oh! fye! Miss Grandison, I wonder how you could think of it!

MISS B. Indeed, Charlotte. I am of Emily's opinion. Are not you, Lady L.?

LADY L. Certainly. And I know my brother will let as few people be by at the ceremony as possible.

[55]

MISS G. I see you are all joined in concert against me, but before I give up, I will take the liberty to chuse how many people I like to be by.

LADY L. I am sure Harriet will not object to that. Shall you Harriet?

MISS B. Oh! not at all. Indeed, I wish myself to have but few people by.

Lord bless me! I do believe here my aunt and cousins come.

MISS G. I suppose Mrs Reeves has brought her marmouset with her.

Enter MR *and* MRS REEVES, MRS SELBY, LUCY *and* NANCY SELBY. MISS BYRON *rising and meeting* MRS SELBY.

MISS B. Oh! how do you do, my dear aunt? How does my grandmamma do?

MRS S. She is pretty well, my love, and she would have come, but she thought the journey too long for her to undertake.

MISS B. Lucy and Nancy, are you quite rid of your colds? And Mrs Reeves! I did not expect this favour.

Let me introduce you all to my friends.

She introduces them.

MISS G. Mrs Reeves, have you not brought your baby?

MR R. No, she would not take that liberty. I wanted her to bring it, because I knew you would excuse it.

Miss Byron, where are the bridegrooms?

LADY L. I will go and call them and my lord.

Exit LADY L.

MISS B. Lucy, were the roads very good?

LUCY. Indeed, they were very good.

MR R. Yes, our ponies went on fast enough.

MISS G. Did you ride, sir?

[56]

MR R. No, ma'am, we came in our phaeton and the Selbys in their coach.

Enter LADY L. *with the four gentlemen. She introduces them.*

MR S. Mrs Selby, here is the bridegroom of your Harriet. Adsheart! we shall have a double marriage, as sure as two and two make four. And here is the other bridegroom.

pointing to LORD G.

MISS G. Yes, that is my man, sure enough. I wish I had a better one to show you. But he is better than he was.

SIR C. Fye! Charlotte, I am sure you have nothing to complain of in Lord G. And if you will make a good wife, I will answer for it, he will a husband.

And I hope you will be as happy as I promise myself Miss Byron and I shall be. And I hope she will have no reason to lament having chosen me for her husband.

The Curtain Falls

TRANSCRIPTION OF THE MANUSCRIPT

KEY TO CONVENTIONS

L. in text; G. in margin = L. written over G. by Jane Austen

Lord L. = added by Jane Austen

Lord L. = added in pencil, not by Jane Austen

Lord L. = added in ink, not by Jane Austen

~~Lord L.~~ = cancelled in ink by Jane Austen

~~Lord L.~~ = cancelled in ink, not by Jane Austen

~~Lord L.~~ = cancelled in pencil, not by Jane Austen

Lord L. = underlined in MS

Manuscript pages have been numbered consecutively for ease of reference. This numbering begins at 'Act the First' and appears in the running headlines.

A line number in the margin indicates a reference to the Notes on the Manuscript, pp. 120 ff.

Facsimile of original title-page for
'Sir Charles Grandison'

Sir Charles Grandison

or

The happy Man,

a Comedy in **6 acts**   4

Dramatis Personae

Men	Women	

Sir Charles Grandison

Harriet Byron

Sir Hargrave Pollexfen   *Miss Jervois*   9

Lady L.

Lord L.   Milliner

Lord G.   Miss Grandison
          Sally   13
          ~~Miss Jervois~~
Mr. Reeves   *Mrs. Selby*   14
          Mrs. Reeves

Mr. Selby   *Miss Selby*
          Mrs. Auberry
~~Dr. Bartlett~~   *Miss Ane Selby*   16

~~Lord L.~~   Bridget   Miss Auberry   17

          Jenny   Miss Sally

Mr. Beacham

          ~~Mrs. Selby~~
          ~~Miss Selby~~   ~~Milliner.~~   21

[61]

1   Act the First.

Scene the First. Mr. Reeves'

House. Enter Mrs. Reeves

& the Milliner at different

doors.

Mrs. R. So, you have brought

      the dresses, have you?   7

Y   Mil. I have brought the young   8

Lady's dress, & Mistress

says you may depend

upon having yours this

Evening.

Mrs. R. Well, ~~but~~ tell her to   13

be sure & bring it.

            have
But let us ~~see~~ the dress   15

that is come.   16

Facsimile of p. 1 of 'Sir Charles Grandison' showing the early hand

2

She takes the Bandbox out

of the Milliner's hands   2

Mil. Have you any other

commands Madam? __

Mrs. R. No. you may go.

Miss Byron & I will ei=   6
= ~~ther~~ come ~~to day or~~ to   7

morrow & pay you.

      Exit Milliner.

Come, I will see whether
       right
she has made it ~~well~~.   11

Oh! but here is Miss By=
       think
=ron coming. I ~~will~~   13

it is but fair to let her see it
~~let her see it first~~.   *fi(rst)*

3 Enter Miss Byron with
a work bag on her arm.
Mrs. R. Here my dear, here
is your dress come. I
hope it will fit, for if
it does not she will
hardly have time to al=
=ter it, ~~for so many~~   8
~~people employ her &~~
~~these fashionable Milliners~~
~~these sort of people are~~
    ~~not very expeditious.~~
     ~~Miss Byron unlocks~~   13
~~the Bandbox & takes out~~
~~the Dress.~~

4

Miss B.   __ We will take it up

stairs if you please & look

at it, for Mr. Reeves is com:

: ing, & we shall have some

of his Raillery.

            Exeunt in an

               hurry.

    Enter Mr. Reeves.

         ~~Scene 2~~   9

Mr. R. So, for once in a way

I have got the coast clear
   Dresses & Band boxes
of ~~Masquerade Dresses~~; &   12

I hope my wife & Miss Byron

will continue to keep their

      Millinery

5 ~~Band boxes & Dresses~~ in their   1

own rooms, or any where

so as they are not in my

way. Why, if I had not had

a little spirit the other day

I should have had them in

my own study. __

         ~~Enter~~ |E|nter Sally.   8

Sally. ~~Is Miss~~ Do you know where   9

Miss Byron is Sir? __

Mr. R. She is up in her own

room I beleive. __

Sally curtseys & go off. __ **6**   1

Mr. R. Sally, Sally. __

       Re-Enter Sally.

Sally. Sir __

Mr. R. Tell Thomas to bring

out the Bay horse.

Sally. Yes Sir.

        Exit Sally.

Mr. R. Well, I must go & get on

my boots — ~~Exit. *& by that*~~   10

& by that time the horse

will be out. __

4.th

7 Scene 3.^d Mr. Reeves' house. 1

Mr. Reeves entering in a great

hurry at one door, & running
                              calls
out at the other, ~~crosses the~~ 4
behind the Scenes.
~~Stage in great agitation.~~ —

John, run all over London

& see if you can find the   see 7

a   Chairm e n or Chair that took 8

Miss Byron. You know what

number it was. _ Thomas,

run for ~~Dr~~ **Mr** Smith directly. 11

He comes in again

in great agitation.   **8**

~~Enter Mrs. Rees~~   2

Enter Bridget.

Brid. ~~My~~ Mistress is rather   4

better Sir, & begs you will

send for ~~Dr.~~/**Mr** Smith.   6

Mr. R. I have, I have.

                    Exit Bridget.   8

       &

[a] ~~Exit~~ Mr. Re|e|ves at a different
                    Mr Reves
doors. __   calls behind the

Scenes __

    William, run to Mr.

9 Greville's Lodgings & if he

is at home __ Stop William,

Come in here: —
                    with William
(He comes in again, takes   4

out his Writing box & writes

a note in great haste.)
                    a
Here William is ~~the~~   7
        Carry it to Mr. Greville's __
note.   Exit William.   8
            Thomas
    Enter ~~a Servant announcing~~   9
Thos.
        ~~Dr.~~/M̭r. Smith, Sir   ▭   10

Mr. R. Shew him up stairs

    to your Mistress.

Enter John.   **10**

John. I cannot find either the

Chair or the Chai⟨rm⟩en Sir.   ⟨?⟩   3

and Wilson is not come within Sir.   4

Mr. R. Well, she must be car=

: ried out into the country

I think. __ You go to Padding:

: ton & tell Thomas to go

to Hampstead, & see if you

can find her, & I will go

to Clapham.   Exit Mr. Reeves.

11

Act the 2^d.   Scene the 1.st

Paddington ~~Colnebrook.~~

~~Enter Miss Grandison & Miss~~

~~Byron.~~ Mrs. Awberry's Parlour.

Enter Miss Byron, ~~pulled~~ in
^dragged^

by Sir Hargrave Pollexfen.

Mrs. Awberry & her two daughters.

Sir Hargrave brings Miss Byron

a seat. Miss Awberry goes

to a closet & takes out a

long cloak, attempts to put

it round Miss Byron. —

Facsimile of p. 11 of 'Sir Charles Grandison' showing
the cancelled page

1   Act 2.^d — Scene 1st.

Paddington —.

Sir   ~~Enter.~~ The Curtain draws up   3

& discovers ~~Sir Hargrave P.~~

Miss Byron, Mrs. Awberry,

~~Miss Awberry.~~   6

Mrs. A. But my dear young

Lady, think what a large

fortune Sir Hargrave has

got, & he intends you

nothing but marriage —

Miss B. Oh! Mrs. Awberry,   12

do you think I can

marry a man whom

I always disliked & now

hate? Is not this your

House? Cannot you fa:

: vour my Escape? —

2
  Mrs. A. My dear Madam

that is impossible without

detection. You know Sir

Hargrave is here & there

& everywhere.

Miss B. My dear Mrs. Awberry

you shall have all the money

in this purse if you will

release me. ———

Sir Hargrave bursts into the

room.

Sir H. Mrs. Awberry I ~~thought~~   12

see you are not to be

trusted with her, you

are so tender-hearted.

And you Madam! ———

He snatches the purse out

of her hand & flings it on

3

the ground. He goes to the

door & calls

Mr —— —— We are ready.   3

Enter a Clergyman & his

Clerk.

Sir H. Miss Awberry you

will be Bridesmaid if you

please. —

He takes hold of Miss Byron's

hand.

Now Madam, all your

purses will not save

you. —

The Clergyman takes a

book out of his pocket.

Miss Byron screams &

faints away. Miss Sally

Awberry runs in.

4

Miss A. Sally, Sally bring

a glass of water directly.

Mrs. Awberry takes out her

Salts & applies them to Miss

Byron's nose. ——

Sir H. — I wish Women were

not quite so delicate,

with all their faints &

fits! ——

Miss Byron revives. Miss

Sally returns with a glass

of water & offers it to Miss

Byron who drinks some.

Mrs. A. What a long time

you have been Child!

If she faints again I shall

send your Sister. —

Sally aside (I am glad
    of it. —

Sir H. Come Sir, we will ⁵

try again. —

Takes hold of Miss Byron's

hand, Miss Awberry goes

behind her.

Clerg: — reads / . Dearly beloved

—

~~Miss B. I see no Dearly~~   7

~~Beloveds here, & I will~~

~~not have any.~~ —

    Miss B

~~She~~ dashes the book out   10

of his hand. —

    picking it up again /

Clerg: Oh! my poor book!

~~He /~~   14

Sir H. Begin again Sir, if

you please. You shall

be well paid for your

trouble.

Clerg — reading again / Dearly

[77]

6
Beloved ~~B~~ —   1

Miss Byron snatches the book
      his
out of ~~the~~ hand & flings   3

it into the fire, exclaiming

Burn, quick, quick. —

The Clerg^{n} — runs to the fire

& cries out

Oh! Sir Hargrave you must

buy me another. —

Sir H. I will Sir, & twenty

more if you will do the

business. — Is the book

burnt? —

Mrs. A. Yes Sir — & we can:

: not lend you one in its

place, for we have lost

the key of the closet where

we keep our Prayerbooks.

7

Sir H.   Well Sir, I ~~will~~ beleive   1

we must put it off for the

present. And if we are not

married in this house we

shall be in mine in the

Forest.

Clerg^n: Then I may go Sir I sup:

: pose. Remember the Prayer

book. —

Sir H.   Yes Sir . **good morning**   10
             Exit Clergyman &
                his Clerk.

Sir H. — I shall be very much

~~to be~~ obliged to you Mrs. A.   14

if you & the young Ladies

will go out of the room for

an instant. I will see

if I cannot reason with

this perverse girl. —

[79]

8 Mrs. A. Here Deb & Sal, come

out.   Exeunt Mrs & Miss As.

⬚L⬚   Miss B.   ⬚O⬚h! do not ~~let me be~~   3

leave me *(above)*

alone with him, let me

go out too.

She runs to the door. Sir H.

follows her. She gets half way

through the door, & he in shutting

it squeezes her. She screams

& faints. He ~~opens~~ carries her   10

away in his arms to a Chair,

& rings the bell violently.

Enter Mrs. A. & her daughters

Sir H. Bring some water di=

=rectly.

Both the daughters go out.

Miss Byron revives, & ex:

: claims, So, I hope you

have killed me at last.   **9**

Re-enter Miss Awberry with

the water. Sir Hargrave takes

the glass & gives it to Miss

B.

Miss B. No I thank you. I

do not want any thing that

can give me life.

Sir H. — Well Miss Awberry

You had better g|et| out the |o| 10

Cloak. It is ~~alm~~ four o'clock   11

& she may as well die in

my house as in yours.

Mrs. A. Shall I order the

Chariot Sir? —

Sir H. If you please Ma'am.

             long
Miss A. takes ~~out~~ a ~~Capuchin~~   17

Cloak out of a Closet and

10

attempts to put it round Miss

B. — Miss B. struggles.

Sir H. I will put it on Miss

Awberry if she will not

let you.

He puts it on.

Sir H. Will you help me lead

her down stairs Miss Awberry?

Miss A. Yes Sir.

They both take hold of

Miss B. – Enter Sally Awberry.

Sally. Can I be of any ser=

=vice Sir? —

Sir H. You may hold the

Candle.

Sally takes the Candle,

Exeunt. —

Act 3ᵈ —   11

Scene 1.   Colnebrook —

Enter Miss Grandison & Miss

Byron.

Miss B. And where is this

brother of yours to whom

I am so much endebted.

Miss G. Safe in St. James's Square

I hope. — But why my dear

will you continue to think

yourself so much endebted to

him, when he only did his

duty?

Miss B. — But what ~~he~~ must   14

he have thought of me in

such a dress? — Oh! these

odious Masquerades!

B   Miss G — La! my dear, what   18

does it signify what he

[83]

12   thinks? He will under:

: stand it all in time. Come

if your stomach pains you,

you had better go to bed again,

Miss B. No, it does not pain

me at all. But how kind

it was in my cousin Reeves

to come & see me.

Miss G. — Yes, he is a very nice

Man. I like him very much.

He disputes charmingly, — I

thought he would have got

the better of me. — Well

but my dear Harriet, you have

had a letter today. How does

my Grandmama Shirley do,

& my Uncle & Aunt Selby

and my Cousins Lucy &

Nancy ? ~~do ?~~ —   **13**   ı

Miss B. They are all very well

I thank you, & my Grandmama

thinks herself under the greatest

obligation to Sir Charles for

being both her & his Harriet's
   for
Deliverer, **for** if he had not ~~prese~~   7
    would
rescued me, she ~~should~~ have   8

died of a broken heart. —

Miss G. — Well really I am very

glad he saved you for both

your sakes. My brother is a
    I always
charming Man. ~~We all wish~~   13
catch him doing some good

~~him to be married but he has~~

action. We all wish him to be married
but h⟨e has⟩ no time for Love. — At

least he appears to have none.

For he is constantly going a:

: bout from one place to another

[85]

14   But what for, we cannot tell.

And we have such a high

respect for him that we never

interfere in his affairs. ~~Nor~~

4

~~do we ever express a wish to know,~~

~~for we are sure that were~~

~~they ever so important if he~~

~~thought we wished to be ac=~~

~~=quainted with them he~~

~~would tell us.~~ — I will return

in a minute. I am going

to fetch my work bag.

Exit Miss G. —

Miss Byron

What an odd Brother is this!

If he is so fond of them, why

should he wish them not

to know his affairs ? —

~~such~~ **15**

~~I wish I had a brother~~ 1

Re-Enter Miss G.

Miss G. — What is the matter Har=

=riet ? What makes you so dull

Child ? — I shall take care not

to leave you by yourself again

in an hurry, if on my return

I am to find these gloomy fits

have taken hold of you.

Come, I will play you your

favourite tune Laure & Lenze

Miss B. I was thinking of Sir
                    But
Hargrave Pollexfen. Be so   13

good as to play my tune.

Miss G. I will directly.

She goes to the Harpsichord

& plays — After she has done

playing she comes to Miss B.

16

& says   1

Come, it is time for you to

go to bed. It is 4 o'clock &

you have been up ever since

12.   Exeunt.

Curtain draws up & discovers

Miss G. reading in the Library.

Miss G. — Well I think this

book would suit Harriet.

But here is ~~our~~ Sir Charles   11

come home I beleive. I

will go & see. Oh! here he

is. —   Enter Sir Charles.

She goes to him. He takes ~~hold~~   16

~~of~~ her hand.

Sir C. No more colds I hope

my dear Charlotte — but

17

above all, how does our
lovely
~~char~~ Charge do?   2

Miss G. Oh! much better. She
got up at
~~has been u~~ 12, & I have   4

but
    just sent her to bed.   5
      I am very glad of it   6
Sir C. — When do you expect Lord

& Lady L. ? —

Miss G. — This Evening, about

six or seven o'clock.
       as soon as that   10
Sir C. Indeed! ~~I am very glad~~

~~of it.~~

     Enter Jenny.

Jen: Miss Byron would be

glad to speak with you Ma'am.

Miss G. Very well, I will come

to her.

Sir C. How is your Cold Jenny?

Jen: Quite well I thank you Sir.

[89]

18

Curtsies & Exit.

Miss G. You will excuse me

for a minute Sir Charles.

I must obey my summons.
                              Exit.   5

~~Sir C. Good Charlotte~~
          Certainly
Sir C. ⌃Well, I must go & speak

to Frederic. Exit. —

Scene 3. —

Curtain draws up & discovers
          & Lady   11
Lord⌃L. & Sir Charles & Miss

G. at Tea. —

Sir C. So my Lord, you have

heard of our new Sister ?

Lord L. — Yes Sir Charles, and

Miss G. by her description

of her, has made me long

to see her. —

Miss G. Frederic, — Take this

to Sir Charles. — (holding

some Tea.)

Sir C. I hope you will not be

disappointed when you see

her. — I might say <u>We,</u> for

I have hardly seen her yet.

Miss G. — I hope you do not

think me a flatterer Sir

Charles.

Sir C. Certainly not my dear

Charlotte.

Lady L. I assure you Char:

: lotte can flatter sometimes.

Miss G. Oh! for shame Caroline

I thought you knew better

than to tell tales. Lord L.

Will you have any more tea?

Lord L. No I thank you Charlotte.

20

Lady L. But Charlotte how do

we come by our new Sister ?

I have not heard that yet.

Miss G. — Well, we will go &

take a walk in the Garden

& talk about it. Frederic

you may take away.

Come Caroline make haste,

or this fit will be off. —

Gentlemen, will you ac꞊

꞊company us ? —

Sir C. Lord L. Will you?

Lord L. Certainly. ~~Ca~~   13

C Sir C. Y̲es, we will go   14

Charlotte. —

Miss G. — Come, make haste

the fit is almost off

                    Exeunt.

[92]

Act 4. — Scene 1.   **21**

Colnebrook.

Curtain draws up & discovers
Lord L.
Sir C. & Miss G. & Miss B. —

Miss G. What an impudent
is   is
fellow Lord G. to make you   6

wait so Sir Charles. — Oh! he

is a poor creature.

Sir C. Have patience my dear

Charlotte. Something most

likely has detained him.

Miss G. Indeed Sir Charles, you

one   are too forgiving. If he   13
                      he would
were to serve me so, I should

not get into favour for some

time. — What say you Har=

: riot ? —

Miss B. — Indeed Miss G. you

[93]

22

are too severe. — Besides, as

Sir Charles says, something

may detain him; & it is

a different thing making

a Lady wait on a Gentle=
              ought to be   6
=man. But here is an end

of your severity, for the

object of it I beleive is come.

I hear him in the Hall.

       Enter Lord G.

Lord G. — I am afraid I have

been making you wait

Gentlemen.

Miss G. — Well, you need not

be afraid any longer, for
   most
you certainly have.   16

Sir C. Fye Charlotte! — I do not

think that was the civillest

23

thing in the world to say.

Lord G. I hope I have not of:

:fended you Madam.

Miss G. Yes you have, for

making my dear brother

wait.

Sir C. — I will not be bribed

into liking your wit Char=

=lotte. — But where is Caroline

all this while? —

Miss G. — She is gone out in

her Chariot with Emily —

but I wonder Sir Charles you

did not enquire after your

favourite Sister before.

Lord L. — I am sure Miss G.

you cannot reproach your

24   brother with partiality. But

Sir Charles is not it time

for us to go out riding? —

If it is not, I am sure Miss

G. might have spared her

severity on Lord G.

Sir C. I assure you Lord L. ~~you~~   7

that I had not forgot it
~~should not have been be=~~
but I think it is too late
~~=forehand with me~~

to go out now. It is 3 o'clock.

Now Charlotte hold your ton=

=gue. I am sure some

raillery is coming out.

He rings the bell.

Miss G. I will not hold my

tongue Sir Charles.

Sir C. Then Charlotte if you

speak, do not let us have

any severity.   25

Miss G. Very well, I will be
good. Harriot what is the
matter, Child ? You look
languid. I will ring the
bell for some Broth for you.
Sir C. Spare yourself that
trouble my dear Charlotte,
I have just rung it.

      Enter Frederic
Sir C. Bring some sand=
=wiches & a bason of broth
~~Frederic.~~ Exit Frederic.   13
Miss G. Harriot, should you
like your broth up in your
own room better ? —
Miss B. If you please.

26

Sir

Miss G. — Well, we will take   1

it up with us.

Enter Frederic with the Sand=

=wiches & the Broth. He sets

it down upon the Table. Exit

Fred. — Miss G. takes the

broth.

Miss G. — Come Harriot. —

Exit Miss B. & Miss G.

Sir C. hands the Sandwiches.

Sir C. — How long Caroline

has been gone! I hope no

more Sir Hargrave Pollexfens

have run away with her &

Emily. —
                    Miss G.   16
          Enter Lady L. & Miss J.

Lord L. goes to meet her, takes

her hand & leads her to a Sopha.

[98]

Miss G. Lord! what a loving   **27**

Couple they are.

Sir C. Charlotte, hold your

tongue.

Lord L. And where have you

been to my dear Caroline?

Lady L. Only shopping. But

Charlotte where is Miss B ?

Miss G. Very safe in her own

room. I always send her

away when she gapes.

Lady L. Poor Creature! I hope

she does not gape too often.

But seriously Charlotte, is she

worse or better? —

Miss G. Law! Lady L. you

are so afraid I shall not

take care of her. — Why, she

28

is just as she is always

is — languid at 3 o'clock.

I beleive it is because Lord

G. always comes about at

that time; & she is so sorry

to see her poor Charlotte pla:

: gued *so!* — **so**

Miss Jervois. — Dear Miss G.

who plagues you? I am sure

Lord G does not.

Miss G. — Emily you do not

know any thing of the mat꞊

꞊ter. You must hold your

tongue till it is your turn

to be called upon. —

Miss J. Well Miss G. I think

it is you who teaze him,

but he will certainly get

the better of you at last.

[100]

1   He did once you know. And I do
                its being   2
not know what you mean by ᵞmy
turn to be
~~being~~ called upon.

Miss G. Why, when it is your turn

to be married. But you had better
                for   6
not get on Lord G.'s
side;   you

will be worsted certainly. But

come is not it time to dress? (looks

at her watch) Dear me! it is but

four.

Lord L. You need not say "But" Char=

=lotte, for you know we are to

dine at ½ after 4. to day.

Miss G. Indeed my Lord, my Lady

did not tell me so. Well, I will

pardon her this time. Come then

Let us go, if it is time.

            Exeunt Ladies.

G.   Lord L. What an odd girl is Charlotte.   19

But you must not despair Lord
            [101]

2 G. I beleive she likes you tho'

she wont own it. I hope Miss

Byron when she is recovered

will have a little influence over

her.

Sir C. Indeed I hope so too. Miss

Byron is a charming young wo:

=man. & I think from ~~the little~~   ^{what} 8

I have seen of her, her mind is

as complete as her person. She

is the happy medium _{between} ~~of~~ Gravity   11

& over liveliness. She ~~can be~~ ^{is} lively   12

or grave as the occasion requires.

Lord G. Indeed she is a ~~charming~~ ^{delightful}   14
young woman, & only Miss G.

can equal her. ~~Sometimes indeed~~   16

[?]   I do |not| mean any offence to   17

Lady L.

Lord L. Indeed my Lord I do not

take it as such. Caroline

is grave, Charlotte is lively   **3**

I am fond of gravity, you most

likely ~~are fond~~ of Liveliness.   3

       a Footman
      Enter ~~Frederic~~   4

| Fred. | | Foot |man. — Dinner is on Table my

Lord. —

Lord L. Very well.   Exit Footman

| ? | Enter | L |ady L. Miss G. Miss   8
B. & Miss J.

Lord L. Dinner is upon Table

my dear Caroline.
                Harriet &
Lady L. Indeed. Come ~~young~~   12

~~L~~ all of you. —

     Exeunt.

    Act 5. Scene 1.

Library at Colnebrook

    Sir Charles & Mr. Selby.

Mr. S. But my dear Sir Charles my

neice is but 18. I never will
              till
allow her to marry she is 22.   20

    [103]

So

4 I shall take her back into Nor: 1

: thamptonshire if you have done

nothing but put such notions

into the girl's head. I had no no=

=tion of my Harriet's coming to

this. And besides Sir C. I never

will allow her to marry you
     della Porretta
till Lady Clementina is mar=   8

=ried. —

Sir C. Mr. Selby that has been my   10

objection for some time to

making my proposals to Miss

B. But yesterday I received

some Letters from Italy in

which they have great hopes

of Lady Clementina's being

soon persuaded to marry.

She wishes me in the same letter

to set her the example by marry:

: ing an English woman.

[104]

I admire Miss Byron
very much, but I will
never marry her against
your consent. And if you
had not told me she was
18, I should have thought
her quite as much as 22.
I do not mean by her looks,
but by her prudence.

Nr. S. Upon my word you
are a fine fellow, you
have done away all my
objections, & if you can
get Harriots consent you
have mine. I hope she
will not be nice, for
if she do not get a hus:
:band now, she never may

I admire Miss Byron 5

very much, but I will

never marry her against

your consent. And if you

had not told me she was

18, I should have thought

her quite as much as 22.

I do not mean by her looks

but by her prudence.

Mr. S. Upon my word you

are a fine fellow, you

have done away all my

objections, & if you can

get Harriot's consent you

have mine. I hope she

will not be nice, for

if she do not get a hus:

: band now, she never may

6   for she has refused all
the young Gentry of our
Neighbourhood. ~~And~~ as to   3
her fortune I will tell you
plainly she has no more than
14,000£.
Sir C. As to her fortune it is
no object to me. Miss Byron
herself is a Jewel of inestima⹂
⹂ble value. Her understanding
more than makes up for
want of fortune. And now if
we can bring Lord G. & my
Sister Charlotte together we
shall have a double wedding.
But I am afraid Charlotte
is too lively for matrimony.

Mr. S. ~~As sure as two & two make~~ **7**   1
~~Oh!~~ Yes,
~~four,~~ your sister is a fine girl,

only she is too nice about an

husband. Adsheart! I hope you

won't have such a plague with

my Harriot, as I had with my

Dame Selby. Well, but it is

three o'clock. I will go & break

it to her. Sir Charles, you may

come & stay at the door till

you are admitted, you know.

Exeunt. —

Scene 2.   Drawing room.

Lady L. Miss G. Miss B. & Miss

J.

Miss G. — There is something

monstrous frightful to be sure

my dear Harriot in marrying

he   a Man that one likes.   19

[107]

8

Lady L. My dear Charlotte, you

overfrown Harriot with your

Raillery. — I dare say you

will feel the same fright when

you marry Lord G. —
                        I will tell you what   6

Miss G. — ~~Who made you L~~

Lady L. — To tell you a secret

I am not likely to marry Lord
                    want to
G. — for I ~~will~~ be married

at home, & my brother will

not consent to it.

Miss J. Oh! fye! Miss Grandison,

I wonder how you could

think of it!

Miss B. Indeed Charlotte. I am

of Emily's opinion. Are not

you Lady L. ?

Lady L. Certainly. And I know

⟦I⟧ ⟦m⟧y brother will let as few **9**   I

people be by at the Ceremony

as possible.

Miss G. I see you are all joined

in concert against me, but

before I give up, I will take

the liberty to chuse how many

people I like to be by. —

Lady L. I am sure Harriot

will not object to that. Shall

you Harriot? —

Miss B. Oh! not at all. In:

: deed I wish myself to have

but few people by. Lord

Bless me! I do beleive here

are my Aunt & Cousins come.

Miss G. I suppose Mrs. Reeves

10   has brought her Marmouset
with her.
Enter Mr. & Mrs. Reeves, Mrs.
Selby, Lucy & Nancy. — —
Miss Byron rising & meeting
Mrs. Selby.
          Oh! how do you do, my
dear Aunt? — How does my
Grandmama do? —
Mrs. S. She is pretty well my
Love, & she would have
come, but she thought the
Journey too long for her to
undertake.
Miss B. Lucy & Nancy are you
quite rid of your colds?
And Mrs. Reeves! — I did
not expect this favour. —

11

Let me introduce you all to

my friends. —

      She introduces them.

Miss G. Mrs. Reeves, have you not   4

brought your Baby? —

Mr. R. No, she would not take

that liberty. I wanted her to   7

it, because I knew you would

excuse it. Miss Byron, where

are the Bridegrooms? —

Lady L. I will go & call them,

& my Lord. — Exit Lady L.

Miss B. Lucy, were the roads

very good? —

Lucy. Indeed they were very

good; & went   16

Mr. R. Yes, our ponies went on

12   fast enough.

Miss G. Did you ride Sir?

Mr. R. No Ma'am, we came

in our phaeton, & the Selbys

in their Coach. —

Enter Lady L. — with the 4.

Gentlemen. She introduces   7

them.

Mr. S. Mrs. Selby, here is the

Bridegroom of your Harriot.

Adsheart! we shall have a

double marriage, as sure as

two & two make four. And

here is the other Bridegroom.

(pointing to Lord G.)

Miss G. Yes, that is my

Man sure enough. I wish,
I had a
~~he were~~ better one to shew   18

13

you. But he is better than he was.

Sir C. Fye! Charlotte, I am

sure you have nothing to

complain of in Lord G. And

if you will make a good

wife, I will answer for it

he will a Husband. — And

I hope you will be as

happy, as I promise my=

=self Miss Byron & I shall

be. — And I hope she will

have no reason to lament

having chosen me for her

Husband. —

The Curtain Falls.

DESCRIPTION OF THE MANUSCRIPT

Perhaps the most striking feature of the manuscript is its scrappiness. This is not a single, continuously written document but is better described as a small collection of papers, made up of five groups of pages, of different shapes and sizes, from different stocks, written at different times. The early sheets are trimmed jaggedly with scissors and dotted with holes where they have been pinned together, first, one supposes, by Jane Austen, later by others into whose possession the manuscript came. From the hasty writing and the careless way in which changes have been made, it looks as if this was the original working text for the play and that some of the alterations to the dialogue and stage-directions were made while 'Grandison' was actually being tried out in rehearsal.

The first group of material is composed of two sheets—the title page and page one; pages two and three—stuck firmly together down the left-hand side to a depth of about $\frac{1}{2}$ in. The sheets come from different stocks. Sheet one measures about $4\frac{1}{16}$ in. × $3\frac{5}{8}$ in. and is irregularly scissor-cut on all four edges. The cutting along the bottom edge has taken away half the bottom line of writing on page one. This is a piece of careless trimming, indicating that the sheet was cut out of a larger sheet. The handwriting on the title-page is relatively immature and may date from the juvenilia period of the early 1790s. The rather formal layout of the page and the slightly calligraphic hand is in the style of the titles and title-pages of the items in the juvenilia notebooks originally composed between about 1789 and 1793 and transcribed later.

Sheet two measures about $4\frac{1}{16}$ × $3\frac{3}{4}$ in. The top edge is straight, the other three irregularly cut. On page three, at the extreme right-hand margin, towards the bottom, there are pen-strokes which begin words; and these show that the present sheet two was once half of a larger sheet.

The second group consists of two sheets folded in half to make pages four to eleven, from the same stock as sheet two of the first group. Both sheets are irregularly trimmed and measure about $3\frac{5}{8}$ × $3\frac{5}{8}$ in. There is part of a watermark on the second sheet, undated and too fragmentary to be identified.

The first and second groups of material are pinned together and have been re-pinned many times.

The third group consists of a gathering of fourteen sheets, regularly trimmed, neatly folded together, and pinned, only once, to make a little booklet of pages measuring $5\frac{15}{16} \times 3\frac{5}{8}$ in. This was Jane Austen's favourite way of preparing her working paper to write on. Although this gives a small page and leads to cramped writing, it was convenient to carry around and easy to put out of sight (following the family story that later, at Chawton Cottage, she slipped her manuscripts under her blotting paper when the servants were about or a visitor expected). The pages are numbered one to twenty-eight. The paper is watermarked with the maker's name, W SHARP, the year 1799, and a coat of arms. The writing is somewhat scrawled, as if dashed off at speed, and certainly very far from the neat and highly legible hand Jane Austen employed for the manuscript notebooks and her letters.

Comparing this section of pages with the first and second groups, one gets a very clear impression of purposefulness in the business-like appearance of the writing and of the manuscript itself; whereas the earlier material seems to be more exploratory, more the remainder of some stops and starts.

The fourth group consists of another neat gathering, two sheets of larger paper, folded in half to make eight pages ($7\frac{3}{16} \times 4\frac{1}{2}$ in.). The first four are numbered one to four, the remaining four are blank and unnumbered. The paper is watermarked with the maker's name, PORTAL & CO and the year 1796. The writing in this section of the manuscript is neat until the beginning of Grandison's speech on page four. For the rest of the page, the hand is scrawled and carries over, in this same style, to the fifth group.

This last group consists of another neat gathering, four sheets, folded in half to make sixteen pages ($5\frac{15}{16} \times 3\frac{5}{8}$ in.). Nine pages, numbered five to thirteen, are written on, the remaining seven pages are blank. This paper is watermarked with the year 1799.

The numbering of the pages was not by Jane Austen but was carried out in pencil in the same childish hand that added '6 acts' to the title-page and scrawled some changes in the text of the play itself. We can be quite definite about this. Not only is the hand unmistakably the same but the pencil was either blunt or had a fault in the graphite which left a distinctive mark, most clearly seen in the middle of page twenty-eight. The numbering was carried out carelessly, without any attempt at neatness or concern for the appearance of the page. On page forty-three, the number '4' is written over the word 'So' which was a late addition, placed in the top left-hand margin. This tells us that whoever numbered the pages had enough interest in the manuscript to carry out this job, but did so inattentively.

Was it the same inattentiveness that led Anna, or whoever it was who then had access to the manuscript, to write '6' rather than '5' on the title-page? The play unquestionably finishes at the end of Act Five, Scene Two and someone who could count to twenty-eight would not make a mistake between five and six! Could there have been a sixth act, added by someone else, possibly Anna? This is feasible. Jane Austen ends her play with the marriage arrangements for Grandison and Harriet, while Richardson's novel has a Volume Seven beyond this point and the sixth act might have covered this ground. There is a precedent for this elsewhere. Anne wrote an additional section to 'Evelyn' in *Volume the Third*, inserting three leaves loosely at the end of the notebook, signing the initials of her married name J. A. E. L. Moreover, the last seven pages of 'Evelyn' and (in the same notebook) the last four of 'Catharine' were not written by Jane Austen. Evidently, other people had access to the juvenilia notebooks and Jane Austen allowed additions to be made. 'Grandison's' absent sixth act could be accounted for in the same way. Later, the additional material could have become separated from Jane Austen's part of the manuscript and so lost to view.

The other puzzle is the absence of a Scene Two in Act One. Although there is a gap in the numbering of the scenes, there is nothing materially missing from the manuscript. On page six, Scene One comes to an end. The other side of the sheet is page seven, beginning Scene Three. In terms of story-continuity, something could be missing, since the action of the play jumps straight from the preparations for the masquerade in Scene One to the agitation in Scene Three when Harriet has failed to return from the ball. The same person who numbered the pages also spotted that Scene Two was missing and wrote in those words at a suitable break on page four. In turn, 'Scene 2' was crossed out in pencil, not by Jane Austen. What further complicates the question is that on page seven, Jane Austen originally wrote 'Scene 4th', changing it to '3d'.

This could be a simple case of misnumbering. There is a similar case in Act Three, where again Scene Two is missing, the change of scene passing unmarked on page twenty-seven. In Act One, the break in continuity accords with Jane Austen's treatment of the *Grandison* story. She makes no attempt to provide a continuous story-line but relies upon her audience's knowledge of what goes on in the novel.

Perhaps the most interesting change on the manuscript is the cancellation of page eleven, discussed in the notes. This comes at the end of the second group of material and it may mark the end of the early writing. Having made two false starts to Act Two, Jane Austen may have put the manuscript aside and only begun the third version, on page twelve, some years later when she was encouraged to continue the play for an actual performance.

Two particular inconsistencies in the manuscript are worth remarking on: the spelling of 'Harriet' and the use of initials for the names of characters. In *Grandison*, 'Harriet' is spelt with an 'e' and Jane Austen follows this in the cast-list and in all occurrences of the name up to page thirty-two (pp. 23, 24, 26, 27). On page thirty-two, the 'o' spelling begins and is used in eight out of the nine occurrences in Acts Four and Five (pp. 36 twice, 37, 44, 46, 47, 48, 51); the one 'e' spelling is on page forty-two. This could indicate a gap between the writing of Act Three and the last two acts. It may also be that Jane Austen was working away from a text of the novel and that she was not concerned about accuracy or consistency in this matter. In her letters, in 1813, she mentions Harriet Byron twice by name, on both occasions with the 'o' spelling (*Letters*, pp. 322, 344).

In *Grandison* members of the aristocracy are referred to only by their initials. Hence Lord and Lady L. and Lord G. This was a convention of epistolary fiction: the letters were supposedly real and so the identity of these lords and ladies was to be respectfully concealed. Jane Austen follows Richardson in this. But she also uses initials for Charlotte Grandison, Harriet Byron, and Grandison in Acts Four and Five: 'Miss G.' (pp. 32, 34, 35, 39 twice, 41); 'Miss B.' (pp. 38, 43); and 'Sir C.' (p. 43). As with the 'o' spelling of 'Harriet', this may indicate a gap in time between the writing of Act Three and the last two acts. The contractions may simply be a saving of time (as in the manuscripts of *The Watsons*, *Persuasion*, and *Sanditon*). Or, it may be that this is a sporadic joke on the convention and that the performers were meant to follow the very letter of the script. There is a single earlier instance: 'Mrs A.' (p. 18).

NOTES ON THE MANUSCRIPT

In these notes, I have tried to provide some explanation for the corrections and changes to the manuscript, where such reconstruction is possible. I have also tried to distinguish between changes made by Jane Austen and those made by more than one unknown 'reviser', sometimes in ink, sometimes in pencil, and sometimes in an obviously childish hand. The cancellations by Jane Austen are usually in a firm, broad pen-stroke, along the line; the rounded, scribbled cancellations are by the revisers.

Page and line numbers refer to the Transcription of the Manuscript, pp. 59-113, the page numbers being those in the running headlines.

Title-page

This was probably the earliest written part of the entire manuscript. The formal layout and the calligraphic hand are in the same mock-serious style that Jane Austen adopted for the title and cast list of 'The Mystery' (*Volume the First*) and 'The First Act of a Comedy' (*Volume the Second*). Neither of these pieces is dated by Jane Austen but we can place them about 1790.

There are puzzles and anomalies here—characters listed who appear in *Grandison* but not in this play, characters unlisted but who do appear in the play, names cancelled and reinstated. It is difficult to say how many people, children and adults, may have made entries and when. All this points to the composition of the play over a number of years and its accessibility to different members of the family.

4. *6 acts* added in pencil, in the same childish hand as the page numbering throughout the manuscript.

9. *Miss Jervois* added in a childish hand. Her name was on the original cast list, at line 13. Possibly, Jane Austen decided to drop the part. Then, when she was working on the play again, after a period of

years, she brought Emily Jervois into Act Four. So this addition may register her reinstatement.

13. *Sally* is not cancelled but accidentally smudged over.

14-16. *Mrs Selby Miss Selby Miss Ane Selby* are all late entries in the childish hand of *Miss Jervois*. They may simply be neater entries for *Mrs. Selby* and *Miss Selby*, in the same hand, squeezed in untidily at the bottom of the page.

16. *Dr. Bartlett* heavily cancelled. Presumably Jane Austen originally planned to include him. As Grandison's spiritual adviser, he has quite an important part in the novel. But later she decided not to write his part, possibly because there were already enough men's roles.

17. Cancels a second entry for *Lord L.*

17-19. *Bridget Jenny Mr Beacham* are later additions. But there is no part in the play for *Mr Beacham*. This point is discussed in the 'Grandison' and "Grandison"' notes.

21. Why was the *Milliner* entered a second time?

Page 1

7-8. Ink-marks are blots picked up from the cancellations to line 7 of the opposite page.

8. The Milliner was to have answered *Yes* to the question from Mrs Reeves.

13. Cancelled for ease of speaking.

15. Pencil literal correction. Mrs Reeves takes the dress, in the band box, without looking at it.

16. Whoever trimmed the bottom edge of the page cut off half this last line.

Page 2

2. 's' accidentally blotted out.

6-7. *ei* blotted out; *ther* first pencilled out, then crossed out in ink.

7. Removes an unnecessary alternative.

11. Reviser's fussy change.

13–14. Reviser's change. Stresses the 'fairness' of showing the dress at once to Harriet Byron.

Page 3

8–12. Removes unnecessary detail. Line 10 written in later.

13–15. Simplifies stage action.
The ink marks at the right-hand margin are the beginning of the words belonging to the other half of the original sheet, from which this page was cut.

Page 4

9. In the absence of a numbered Scene Two, the reviser thought this the right place to mark its beginning. A later reviser disagreed and pencilled it out.

12. Two items, rather than one, for Mr Reeves to complain about!

Page 5

1. Avoids repetition of corrected phrase on 64. 12.

8. Change of mind? *Enter S*(ally) written. *Enter* cancelled. Then begun again from 'S'.

9. Sally's question re-phrased more politely, more euphoniously.

Page 6

1. A grammatical inconsistency: *go* is a stage direction, in the imperative mood, while *curtseys* is in the indicative.

10. This change could have been made with the young collaborator working alongside Jane Austen in reviewing this early section of the manuscript. First, the scene ended with the *Exit* of Mr Reeves. The collaborator scribbled over *Exit* and began to continue the sentence; and then asked Jane Austen to take over, scribbling over the three words so far written and leaving her to continue. The continuation merely adds a trivial circumstantial detail.

Page 7

1. A puzzle. Why was *Scene 4th* changed to *3d* when there is no Scene Two? Did Jane Austen suppose that she had already made a scene-change on page 65 where Mrs Reeves and Harriet Byron leave and Mr Reeves enters? Or is there really a missing scene, written on loose pages?

4-5. The original stage direction merely repeats lines 2-4. The correction introduces a specific action.

7. Avoids the repetition of *see*.

8. Literal correction. One man could not carry a chair.

11. Reviser decides that *Dr* is incorrect. Substitutes *Mr*, indicating a surgeon or apothecary.

Page 8

2. *Rees* by mistake for *Reeves*. The cancellation then creates an additional small speaking-part.

4. Cancelled by Jane Austen and scribbled over in pencil. Was Jane Austen's cancellation to confirm the collaborator's attempt to improve the speakability of these lines?

6. As page 7, line 11.

8-10. Jane Austen had Bridget exiting first, followed by Mr Reeves. The reviser changes the directions, carelessly, so that they now exit simultaneously, but still at *a . . . doors*.

Page 9

4. Reviser's literal correction.

7. Reviser's fussy correction.

8. Added to emphasize instructions.

9. Creates an additional named speaking-part.

10. As page 68, line 11.

Page 10

3. To correct mispenning.

4. This line written in slightly later.

Page 11

From this cancelled page, we can see that Jane Austen's original intention was that the play should continue in Lord L.'s house at Colnebrook, with Charlotte Grandison and Harriet Byron. Having got as far as writing down the two names and the location, she seems to have changed her mind, at that very point, recommencing the act in Mrs Awberry's house with a long and elaborate stage direction. Evidently, at this moment, Jane Austen had not devised the attempted marriage ceremony and if she had continued the play along these lines, the action would have begun at the present page eighty-two.

The abandoned Colnebrook opening becomes Scene One of the third Act.

Page 12

Comparing pages eleven and twelve, on the latter page we see a firmer, slightly more decisive hand and a more economical form of act and scene numbering. These differences suggest that a period of time elapsed between the writing of the cancelled page and the fresh start on page twelve. It may have been that Jane Austen lost interest in the play at this point, with the two false starts to the second Act, then put the manuscript aside and brought it out again later when prompted by the call for a family play.

3. The original stage direction was to have been *Enter Sir Hargrave Pollexfen*. Jane Austen probably cancelled the name when she realized that the dramatic effect would be heightened if he were to be positioned off-stage yet visible to the audience and overhearing Harriet's attempt to bribe Mrs Awberry.

6. A puzzling cancellation, since Miss Awberry is required on stage.

12. An ink-blot obscures *Oh*!.

[124]

Page 13

12. Jane Austen was probably going to continue *I thought you were to be trusted*. The change makes Pollexfen's accusation more emphatic.

Page 14

3. Jane Austen left a space for the clergyman's name—so that the name of a local clergyman could be inserted for the actual performance?

Page 16

7–9. A good joke cancelled. Why?—because it trod rather heavily on clerical ground and might be thought to be in bad taste?

10. With the cancellation of *Miss B* in line 7, this change, in a childish reviser's hand, is sensible.

13. Jane Austen began the stage direction *He picks up the book*, but abandoned it, writing in instead the stage-direction between lines 11 and 13.

Page 17

1. Was the clergyman to have continued *Bretheren*?

3. Simple verbal error. Was Jane Austen thinking ahead to *the fire*?

Page 18

1. Probably Jane Austen was going to continue *I will put it off* . . . and then changed to a more formally polite phrasing.

10. Reviser's addition of a polite farewell.

14. Careless mistake.

Page 19

3. Did Jane Austen begin *Ladies!*, discarding that for a more emphatic cry?

10. Pollexfen was to open the door, but Jane Austen makes him first attend to Harriet.

14. Superfluous words cancelled; makes for easier speaking.

Page 20

10. Reviser's correction of Jane Austen's literal mistake.

11. Jane Austen begins to write *almost*, then removes this unnecessary qualification.

17. In writing this stage-direction, Jane Austen decides to place the preposition later in the sentence. In *Grandison*, Pollexfen has two cloaks for Harriet Byron, a capuchin and a long man's cloak. Here we see Jane Austen opting for the long cloak alone.

Page 22

From changes in the style of the handwriting, it looks as if there was a break between Jane Austen's completion of Act Two and the beginning of Act Three.

14. Jane Austen begins to write *what he must have thought of me*, inverting this to *must he* to heighten the note of anxious uncertainty in Harriet's question.

18. Corrects a literal error.

Page 24

1. Removes a superfluous word.

7. Reviser adds a conjunction to ease the flow of the sentence and bring out the sequence of cause and effect. It looks as if Jane Austen then endorsed this change by writing in *for* herself above the reviser's pencilled word.

Jane Austen begins to write *preserved*; then changes to *rescued* because this conveys more forcefully what Grandison actually did in the novel: in answering Harriet's cry for help as she is being carried away in Pollexfen's coach to his house in Windsor Forest, pulling him out of the coach and carrying her 'in his arms' to the safety of his own coach (1. 33).

8. Regularizes the verb form to accord with *if*.

13–16. Jane Austen inserts a new sentence and rearranges the material,

[126]

introducing a reference to Grandison as a doer-of-good-deeds, alluding to his character in the novel as an exemplary social hero whose Christianity is active in his everyday life and dealings with other people.

Page 25

4-10. A rather wandering and undramatic sentence, difficult to speak, whose import is already carried by the previous sentence—and so cancelled?

Page 26

1. Jane Austen intended to continue Harriet's reflections on Grandison: first, probably, along the lines of 'I wish I had a brother so good . . .'. Then she curtailed it, neatly, to *such a brother*. Difficult to guess why she removed the line; because it clashed with the idea of his being an *odd brother*?

13. Addition of adversative conjunction fits the sense of these two sentences.

Page 27

1. After *says*, a heavy ink-spot.

11. Jane Austen begins to write *our brother*; cancels, preferring, for dramatic effect, the actual name.

16-17. Reviser fussily removes superfluous words.

Page 28

2. Jane Austen begins to write *charge* unqualified; then inserts the appropriate courtesy-epithet which, Grandison, the perfect gentleman would unfailingly produce. Moreover, in *Grandison* Harriet is celebrated for her beauty: 'She is all loveliness' declares Greville, one of her many admirers, in the novel's second letter and continues with a minute elaboration over the next three pages!

4. Jane Austen starts to write *has been up since twelve*. Change to achieve a sharper, more colloquial style?

5. Added *but* later to emphasize the length of time Harriet has been up.

6. Reviser takes this sentence from Grandison's lines 10–11 and replaces it there with an expression of surprise.

10. Reviser wrote *that* with a bad/blunt? pencil, so the *t* did not show up clearly; then rewrote *that* above it.

Page 29

5–6. Jane Austen cancels Grandison's words of acknowledgement and farewell to his sister, gives him a final remark and then reinstates the acknowledgement and farewell in *Certainly*.

11. Consistency correction. Lady L. is in this scene.

Page 31

13. Lord L. was going to continue with his wife's name.

14. Grandison was probably going to begin with his sister's name.

Page 32

6. Correction of omission.
Jane Austen first writes the line without an *is*; reviser inserts one; then Jane Austen inserts it in a preferred position. Or did Jane Austen first make good the omission and then the reviser add the second *is* in pencil?

14–15. Originally, Charlotte was to explain what she would do if someone unspecified were late. The change now attaches the threat to Lord G.

Page 33

6. The change turns Harriet's statement into a light reprimand.

16. Reviser's addition enables Charlotte to score off Lord G. more heavily.

Page 35

7–10. At first, Grandison politely reassures Lord L. that his reminder could not be premature. Then Jane Austen makes his reply more definite and less circumlocutory.

Page 36

13. Reviser judges the servant's name unnecessary.

Page 37

1. Jane Austen begins to write *Sir* but changes mind and gives the next words to Grandison's sister.

16. Charlotte has just left with Harriet; as an afterthought, Jane Austen brings her back to continue the play of her wit upon the assembled company.

Page 39

1–2. There is an *is* too many. Probably the second one in line one would have been cancelled in a careful revision.

7. It looks as if the reviser added *so* for emphasis and that Jane Austen consented to the suggestion, confirming it in ink. She would not have initiated this addition herself, since she had already used 'so' only two lines before.

Page 40

This last gathering appears to be less scribbled than the previous one. But this may represent the benefit of a larger page and a different pen, rather than anything more significant, such as an appreciable gap in the period of writing.

2–3. The change repeats Charlotte's wording more accurately.

6. As on page 85, the reviser adds a conjunction to ease the sentence flow, and emphasize cause and effect.

19. Jane Austen begins to write *Lord G.* Then she probably felt it more in character for Lord L. to pass a comment on Charlotte's behaviour.

Page 41

8. Reviser adds an ampersand for continuity. An appropriate change, if Grandison is going to pass an opinion based upon sound judgement; 'the little I have seen of her' might cast a doubt upon that.

11. Jane Austen finds a slightly more fitting word to complement *medium.*

12. *is* suggests that the mood-changes are effortless.

14. Jane Austen notices that Grandison has just said *charming young woman* a few lines before and prefers an elegant variation to an emphatic repetition.

16. Presumably Lord G. was to continue his praise more extravagantly, to the effect that in certain respects Harriet is unequalled. Jane Austen decides to cut this short; also to avoid the repetition of *indeed.*

17. *not* written over an indecipherable word.

Page 42

3. Reviser cancels for compression and neatness.

4–5. Jane Austen takes the opportunity to create an additional part.

8. *L* written over an indecipherable letter—*H*?

12. Lady L. begins to say *young Ladies*; mentions Harriet because she accompanies her off the stage?

20. Corrects omission.

Page 43

1. *So* is an addition—Jane Austen's? The reviser's? It became blotted out, probably accidentally. Then, carelessly, the page-numberer wrote *4* in pencil over it.

8. The formality of the full family name is more correct on such an occasion.

10. The change of hand and change of pen are obvious at this point and probably mark a break in the continuity of writing.

Page 44

> This gathering, judging from the decisiveness and speed of the writing, was the last written. The spelling *Harriot* suggests that Jane Austen was not over-concerned with consistency, since there is *Harriet* on page 104. The final two pages appear even more hurriedly written, as if Jane Austen was really rushing to complete the play.

Page 45

3. Why did the reviser scribble out *And*? Could this be an improvement made when the lines were being tried out aloud for performance? This would make Grandison's repetition of the words, at the beginning of next speech, an exact repetition, and allow the actor to indulge in a heavily ironic voicing.

Page 46

1-2. Mr Selby bursts out with an emphatic saying. Jane Austen may have cancelled it on re-reading the play, to avoid the repetition of these words on page 112. She replaced them with the mild and unremarkable *Oh! Yes* . . . which the reviser has toned down even more, to a mere *Yes* . . . .

19. Correction of verbal error.

Page 47

6. Charlotte begins an offensive retort to Lady L., probably along the lines of *Who made you think that I will marry Lord G.*?

9. Change turns the certainty into a wish; also avoids *will* in successive lines.

Page 48

1. Lady L. was to have said what she wanted. But Jane Austen changes this to convey her opinion of Grandison's wishes instead.

Page 50

4. Jane Austen changes the speaker. *Miss G.* a late addition, squeezed in.

7. Word omitted: *bring* needed to complete the sense. The fact that this omission could survive uncorrected suggests that the revision of the manuscript was not careful and systematic, as would be the case if this was one of Jane Austen's serious literary manuscripts. What we seem to have instead is sporadic, piecemeal correction such as one would expect to see on the manuscript of a play written for performance and which went through the hands of children.

16. Lucy was to have enlarged upon the pace of the ponies. Jane Austen cancels her beginning and starts again, with Mr Reeves putting in the change of subject.

Page 51

7. The stage direction originally ended at *Gentlemen*. The additional instruction belongs to an acting text.

18. Charlotte is made even more bossily possessive.

GRANDISON AND 'GRANDISON'

Page references to Jane Austen's manuscript follow the pagination shown in the running headlines.

Reference to Richardson's *Grandison* is by volume number and letter number, following the text of the authoritative Oxford edition, edited by Jocelyn Harris (1972).

Title-page

The happy Man. i.e. The happily married man; see Grandison's declaration, 'I shall not think myself happy till I can obtain the hand of a worthy woman' (3. 15).

The marriage-happiness association is a verbal motif. Pollexfen calls himself 'an happy man' when he learns that Harriet is free to make her own choice in marriage (1. 14). In proposing, Grandison entreats Harriet to make him 'soon the happy husband' (6. 27); Clementina wishes him 'soon the happy man' (6. 34); and Grandison describes himself to Harriet as 'the happy man' (6. 40). There are also the familiar phrases about the 'happy day' (6. 29, 40), 'the happy pair' (6. 33), 'happy tidings', and 'happy prospects' (7. 44). Jane Austen's use of the phrase in the play's subtitle is discussed in the Introduction, page 22.

Dramatis Personae. Richardson places the 'Names of the Principal Persons' under three heads: Men   Women   Italians.

Lord L.   Lady L.   Lord G. The contracted forms are in *Grandison* and Jane Austen follows Richardson in keeping to these initials throughout the play. See Description of the Manuscript, pp. 118-119.

Dr. Bartlett. A clergyman who plays an important role as Grandison's spiritual adviser and confidant.

Mr. Beacham. An English phonetic spelling for Beauchamp, of French origin. At this stage, then, it seems that Jane Austen was not working from a text of the novel but was relying on her memory; hence the sound of the name, rather than its spelling, came first to mind.

dearest friend . . . a second Sir Charles Grandison' (2. 37). He is destined to marry Emily Jervois.

Presumably Jane Austen originally planned to have this couple in 'Grandison', since Emily is given a small but lively part. But this intention seems to have been abandoned or forgotten as Mr Beacham does not appear.

Mrs. Auberry. Widow Awberry. Jane Austen uses the 'w' spelling within the play.

Milliner. Does not appear in *Grandison*.

Act the First. Scene the First

Mrs Reeves is a cousin in Harriet, living in Grosvenor Street, where Harriet stays when she first comes to London.

This scene has no direct source in *Grandison* and is discussed in the Introduction, pp. 22-3.

Page 4. Raillery. See Introduction, pp. 23-4. Mr Reeves's 'Raillery' and the 'spirit' he credits himself with (page 5) really belong to Richardson's Mr Selby, whom Harriet sometimes tries to avoid: 'I am only afraid of my uncle. He will railly his Harriet; yet only, I know, in hopes to divert her, and us all: But my jesting days are over: My situation will not bear it' (4. 24; her 'situation' is a delicate one, regarding Grandison). Mr Selby's favourite tirade runs on *'shilly shally's* and *fiddle-faddles*, and the rest of our *female nonsenses*, as he calls them' (6. 17, Harriet to Lady G.; see also his lengthy outburst to his wife, 6. 25).

Page 7. Scene 3d. In the manuscript, the play jumps from the preparations for the masquerade directly to the events following it. In between, in *Grandison*, Harriet has been abducted in her chair to Mrs Awberry's house in Paddington; and this scene shows the upset at the Reeves' house when Harriet fails to return from the masquerade.

Jane Austen bases the scene on a letter from Mr Reeves to Mr Selby (1. 23) in which he reports all he knows of these events and the state of the household:

Dear Mr SELBY,—No one, at present, but yourself, must see the contents of what I am going to write.

You must not be too much surpris'd.

But how shall I tell you the news; the dreadful news?—My wife has been ever since three this morning in violent hysterics upon it.

You must not—But how shall I say, *You* must not, be too much affected, when *we* are unable to support ourselves?

Oh, my cousin Selby!—We know not what is become of our dearest Miss Byron!

I will be as particular as my grief and surprize will allow. There is a necessity for it, as you will find.

Mr. Greville, as I apprehend—But to particulars first.

We were last night at the Ball in the Hay-market.

The chairmen who carried the dear creature, and who, as well as *our* chairmen, were engaged for the night, were inveigled away to drink somewhere. They promised Wilson, my cousin's servant, to return in half an hour.

It was then but little more than twelve.

Wilson waited near two hours, and they not returning, he hired a chair to supply their place . . .

Jane Austen catches the breathless style of this letter in Mr Reeves's agitation on stage. Later in the letter there is a single sentence—'I have six people out at different parts of the town, who are to make inquiries among chairmen, coachmen, etc'—which Jane Austen elaborates, dramatically, into Mr Reeves giving orders to John, William, and Thomas (none of whom are in *Grandison*).

His orders to John derive from another part of this letter: 'I have sent after the chairmen who carried her to this cursed masquerade. Lady Betty's chairmen, who had provided the chairs, knew them and their number.'

Mr Smith. Not in *Grandison*.

Page 9. *Greville.* One of Harriet's most persistent and unwelcome admirers from her home neighbourhood in Northamptonshire. Mr Reeves suspects that she may have been taken to his lodgings, since Greville has come to London to press his case, has been lurking around, threateningly, and was seen at the masquerade. These circumstances are explained at length in Mr Reeves's letter to Mr Selby (1. 23), to this conclusion, 'I think it is hardly to be doubted, but Mr. Greville is at the bottom of this black affair.'

Page 10. *Wilson*. William Wilson plays an important part in the abduction. He is bribed by Pollexfen to enter Harriet's service as a footman, to make the chairmen drunk and get the chair to Widow Awberry's house. At this point in the play, as in the novel (1. 23), Mr Reeves does not suspect him.

Act 2.^d Scene 1st.

Page 12. This scene is loosely based upon a sequence of letters (1. 29-33) in which Harriet gives her account of these misadventures to her confidante Lucy Selby. Having swooned, she comes to and finds herself in Mrs Awberry's house, attended by her and her two daughters. After some conversation, Pollexfen bursts in, dismisses the three women and threatens Harriet darkly on the dire consequences of her not marrying him: 'Be mine, madam. Be legally mine . . . or take the consequence . . . Don't provoke me: Don't make me desperate' (1. 29). Here, and later, when Harriet resists going through a ceremony of marriage with him, Richardson serves up a series of suggestive hints as to her fate-worse-than-death, 'ruin' itself (1. 29), if she continues to refuse him.

large fortune and *marriage*. Mrs Awberry assures Harriet: 'No ruin is intended you. One of the richest and noblest men in England is your admirer. He dies for you. He assures me, that he intends honourable marriage to you' (1. 29). Again, after Harriet has halted the clergyman: 'Can you have a man of greater fortune? Sir Hargrave means nothing but what is honourable' (1. 31).

disliked & now hate. This refers back to Harriet's earlier acquaintance with Pollexfen. He fancies himself as a highly eligible match. 'rakish' and 'very voluble' (1. 11), he supposes that Harriet will come running, drawn by his looks, his money, and his title. But she finds him bumptious and vain and tells him 'the simplest truth', that he does not 'hit' her 'fancy' (1. 17).

Escape 'and began to pray, to beg, to offer rewards if they would facilitate my escape' (1. 29). After the attempted marriage, she offers £1,000; and, as in the play, Pollexfen bursts in (1. 33).

Page 13. *here & there & everywhere.* This comic notion is a reference to the succession of inexplicable entrances and exits that Pollexfen, like a real stage villain, makes within the space of a paragraph (1. 29, 31).

Page 14. *Clergyman.* Richardson's clergyman is unnamed. He is a grotesque, Hogarthian creature, described graphically: 'A vast tall, big-boned, splayfooted man. A shabby gown; as shabby a wig; a huge red pimply face; and a nose that hid half of it' (1. 30).

faints. Richardson's heroine screams and is twice on the verge of fainting but on both occasions is revived with hartshorn and water (1. 29, 31).

Page 15. *faints & fits.* Pollexfen remarks, 'I thought that the best of you all could fall into fits and swoonings whenever you pleased . . . Can't you go into fits again? Can't you . . . now fall into fits again' (1. 32).

'Fits' are a feature of the first volume of *Grandison*. Harriet suffers a succession of them at Paddington, on the way to Windsor Forest, and during her convalescence at Colnebrook. Moreover, during the middle sections of the novel, Clementina exhibits the whole gamut of women's nervous and hysterical conditions. Richardson was fascinated by the subject and was well equipped to write about it, since he was the publisher of two important treatises, *The English Malady* (1733) by George Cheyne and the *Medical Directory* (1743–5) by Robert James. Undoubtedly, he meant them to be taken seriously in *Grandison*. But it would call for much less than Jane Austen's sense of the ridiculous to see the unconscious humour of Harriet's account of the events at Paddington: 'I was in a perfect frenzy; but it was not an unhappy frenzy; since, in all probability, it kept me from falling into fits; and fits, the villain had said, should not save me' (1. 31); and William Wilson wonders 'how she kept out of fits on the road. She had enow of them at Paddington' (1. 35).

glad of it. Meaning, perhaps, that she is glad not to be further involved. In the novel, Harriet supposes the other, younger sister to be 'more tender-hearted than the elder' (1. 32) and she answers Harriet's questions with 'compassionate frankness' (1. 32).

Page 16. *Takes . . . hand.* Cf. 'Sir Hargrave took my struggling hand' (1. 30).

Dearly beloved. Cf. Harriet's account: '*Dearly beloved*, began to read the snuffling monster' (1. 30). She succeeds in wresting the prayer-book out of his hand; he makes a second attempt, '*Dearly beloved*, again snuffled the wretch'. She tries unsuccessfully to grab the book, but Pollexfen stops her, and she is left to utter the memorable cry, 'No *dearly beloved's*', which Pollexfen mockingly repeats (1. 31).

Page 17. The throwing of the prayer-book into the fire and the lost key are Jane Austen's invention.

Page 18. *Forest*. Pollexfen has a house in Windsor Forest.

Pages 19–20. The sequence of action and some of the dialogue is in *Grandison*. Harriet tries to follow the three women out of the door: 'but the wretch, in shutting them out, squeezed me dreadfully, as I was half in, half out; and my nose gushed out with blood. I screamed . . . So, so, you have killed me, I hope—Well, now I hope, now I hope, you are satisfied' (1. 31).

Page 20. *Well . . . Cloak*. 'Pray, Miss Sally, put on this lady's capuchin' (1. 32). Sally is the elder Awberry daughter; in 'Grandison' she is the younger.

chariot. This is the style of carriage named in *Grandison* (1. 32). It was a light, four-wheeled vehicle, with all the seats facing the front.

Pages 20–1. *Capuchin* (cancelled). Richardson makes a considerable business about this capuchin-cloak: Pollexfen's insistence that Harriet put it on, her resistance, which he counters by holding her tightly while Sally Awberry wraps it round her. He throws a long, red, man's cloak over it (1. 32).

A capuchin was a woman's cloak, with a hood, so named because it resembled the robes of the Capuchin Order. It was a form of concealing dress popularly associated with intrigues, assignations, elopements, and other such scandalous goings-on.

Page 21. *candle*. Sally Awberry stands at the door of the house with a lighted candle (1. 32).

Act 3ᵈ. Scene 1

Page 22. Colnebrook, west of London, is the home of Lord and Lady L., where Harriet is brought by Grandison after the rescue. Lady L. is his elder sister.

endebted. Harriet's sense of 'gratitude' to Grandison is, in time, 'exalted' 'into love' (2. 10).

such a dress. Harriet is in agonies of shame and embarrassment about being rescued in her masquerade dress. An innocent in these matters, she allowed herself to be arrayed in what was, in fact, a compromising garment. Masquerades were notorious as places for sexual adventures; they were the haunt of prostitutes; and, as Harriet discovers too late, she is in danger of being seriously misjudged. Her companions go dressed as á hermit, a nun, and a lady abbess; she goes as 'an Arcadian princess' (a favourite masquerade costume), in a costume which is gaudy, glittering, and elaborately decorated. She describes it at length, with a sense of uneasiness, before going to the ball (1. 22). Having been rescued by Grandison, after the ball, she now appreciates how compromising it really is and feels compelled to exculpate herself before Grandison and Charlotte: 'You see before you, madam, said she, a strange creature, and look'd at her dress: but I hope you will believe I am an innocent one. This vile appearance was not my choice. Fie upon me! I must be thus dress'd out for a Masquerade: Hated diversion! I never had a notion of it. Think not hardly, Sir, turning to Sir Charles, her hands clasped and held up, of her whom you have so generously delivered. Think not hardly of me, madam, turning to me: I am not a bad creature. That vile, vile man! and she could say no more' (1. 26).

The subject is given another, extensive airing when Charlotte, 'in her lively way . . . led me into talking of the detested masquerade. She put me upon recollecting the giddy scene . . . What were Sir Charles's first thoughts of me, Lucy, in that fantastic, that hated dress?' There follows a lengthy discussion about the moral pros and cons of masquerades. This is dramatic in form, didactic in intention, and provides a conduct-book style of instruction for the young reader (2. 31a).

these odious Masquerades. The mask-and-costume ball that Harriet goes to is at the Haymarket Opera House. Their odiousness is explored in the previous note. Cf. 'These cursed masquerades' (1. 25, Mr Reeves), 'that odious masquerade habit' (i.e. dress; 1. 36).

Charlotte's dismissive comment is quite in character and echoes her part in the discussion referred to above, at 2. 31a.

Page 23. cousin Reeves. He visits Colnebrook on 18 February at 9.00 a.m., Harriet having been abducted in the early hours of the 17th.

disputes charmingly. Richardson's Mr Reeves is incapable of disputing with anyone, 'charmingly' or otherwise! The nearest he gets to disagreement with Charlotte is when she enquires, on the morning of his visit, if he has had breakfast: 'Have you breakfasted, sir? Breakfasted, madam! My impatience to see my cousin allowed me not to think of breakfast. You must breakfast with me, Sir. And when that is over, if she is tolerable, we will acquaint her with your arrival, and go up together. I read your impatience, sir: we will make but a very short breakfasting. I was just *going* to breakfast. She rang. It was brought in.' (1. 26).

Richardson develops the comedy of the bullying Charlotte and the bullied Mr Reeves in the next letter, when he tries to leave before dinner: 'I answered for you, that you would stay dinner. I must beg excuse, madam. I have an excellent wife. She loves Miss Byron as her life: She will be impatient to know—Well, well, well, say no more, Mr Reeves: My brother has redeemed one prisoner, and his sister has taken another: and glad you may be that it is no worse. I bowed, and look'd silly, I believe.' (1. 27).

This is an aspect of the Richardsonian battle-of-the-sexes comedy that Jane Austen admired and profited from, observing the neatness and precision of the phrasing and wit, and the element of the ridiculous in Mr Reeves's predicament.

Remembering these exchanges, the audience must have roared with laughter when they heard Charlotte confessing modestly that she 'thought he would have got the better of me'!

my Grandmama etc. Charlotte speaks possessively of Harriet's relatives, since she now treats her as a member of the Grandison family. The wording of her question is a burlesque version of Harriet's lamentations about them, which Charlotte cuts short: 'Oh my poor Grandmamma—Oh my good Aunt Selby, and my Lucy—I hope—Miss Grandison interposed, humorously, interrupting—I will have nothing said that begins with *O*' (reported by Mr Reeves, 1. 26). Later, Charlotte mimics Harriet: 'But Mr Reeves told me that you are a writer; and that you give a full account of all that befell you to *our* grandmother Shirley, to *our* uncle and aunt Selby, to *our* cousins Lucy and Nancy—You see I remember every name . . .' (1. 37).

Page 24. *Deliverer*. Cf. 'A man's voice (it was my deliverer's . . .' (1. 33); 'But now for her brother—my deliverer!' (1. 36).

broken heart. There are several pathetic references to the 'poor grandmother' (1. 23), 'Fatal news indeed! It will be immediate death to her poor grandmother' (1. 24). The explanation for this cautiousness, and the need to keep from her the news of Harriet's disappearance, are in 1. 26, from Harriet to Lucy Selby, in which the grandmother appears as a scaremongering Mrs Morland: 'My grandmamma has told us girls, you know, my Lucy, twenty and twenty frightful stories of the vile enterprises of men against innocent creatures; and will therefore call to mind stories that have concluded much worse than, blessed to God! mine has done.'

good action. Cf. 'his whole delight is in doing good' (Dr Bartlett, 3. 12). In *Grandison*, the hero's goodness is essentially an active Christian virtue and Richardson explains in his 'Concluding Note' that Grandison is proposed to us to exemplify 'what a degree of excellence may be attained and preserved amidst all the infection of fashionable vice and folly.' In *Grandison*, it is given to Charlotte to speak most eloquently of his goodness: 'My brother is valued by those who know him best, not so much for being an handsome man; not so much for his birth and fortune; nor for this or that single worthiness; as for being, in the great and yet comprehensive sense of the word, a *good man*' (1. 36). These sentiments are backed up by Harriet: 'I have met with persons, who call those men *good*, that yet allow themselves in liberties which no good man can take. But I dare say, that Miss Grandison means by *good*, when she calls her brother, with so much pride, *a good man*, what I, and what you, my Lucy, would understand by the word' (1. 36).

we . . . married . . . Love. Harriet reports to Lucy Selby that Charlotte and Lady L. 'said they were extremely solicitous to see their brother married' (2. 31). Lady L. tells Dr Bartlett that 'we are so very desirous to see my brother happily married' (2. 33); and Charlotte tells Grandison himself 'that we long to have you happily married' (3. 15).

going about. Geographically, Grandison is a world traveller! In addition to the 'tour of Europe . . . He has visited some parts of Asia, and even of Afric, Egypt particularly' (1. 36). His mysterious trips to Canterbury may come into this: 'his journeying thither backward and forward' (2. 6). 'I go to different places, and return, and hardly think it worth troubling my sisters with every movement' (2. 28). This is Grandison in the character of the cultivated English gentleman who thinks nothing of great journeys and urbanely regards the world as his parish. Richardson elevates him above mere run-of-the-mill tourist curiosity and connoisseurship, and credits him with a truly extraordinary readiness to oblige: 'Seas are nothing to him. Dr Bartlett said, that he considers all nations as joined on the same continent; and doubted not but if he had a call, he would undertake a journey to Constantinople or Pekin, with as little difficulty as some others would (he might have named me for one) to the Land's-End' (Mr Deane to Mrs Selby, 3. 6).

His ubiquity also runs to mundane, homely settings, such as a family party: 'Sir Charles was everywhere, and with everybody' (7. 7).

Richardson presses these aspects of Grandison's superhumanism to extravagant lengths and they provide a ready target.

Page 25. *But what for . . . his affairs.* Another slightly ridiculous aspect of Grandison is the element of mystery that surrounds his affairs, as if they are to be veiled from the curiosity of ordinary men. One very curious person is Charlotte. She resents her brother's reserve and secrecy. She suggests that this concealment is a defect, a question which Harriet ponders deeply (1. 36). Charlotte admits that 'he sometimes loves to play with my curiosity' (1. 37). Harriet develops this idea: 'Charlotte accuses her brother of reserves. I never found him reserved: But he loves to play with her curiosity, and amuse her' (2. 6).

Grandison plays a cat-and-mouse game with his sister: 'Sometimes, indeed, I love to divert myself with Charlotte's humorous curiosity; for she seems, as I told her lately, to love to suppose secrets, where there are none, for a compliment to her own sagacity, when she thinks she has found them out; and I love at such times to see her puzzled, and at a fault, as a punishment for her declining to speak out', he confides to Dr Bartlett (3. 4).

work bag. Charlotte's work-bag makes an amusing appearance towards the end of the novel. In a conversation with her husband, she refers to it sarcastically several times: 'Now I intend to put up all our little quarrels in my work-bag', in order to produce them 'one by one' to place before the company when they go to visit Harriet and her relatives (5. 11).

What . . . affairs. For Harriet, the question is raised extensively in 1. 36 and 37, in particular, regarding Charlotte: 'I cannot excuse him, if he be guilty of a difference and reserve to his generous sister' (36). The 'odd Brother' reflection stems from such thoughts as 'But once more, I wonder why a man of a turn so laudable, should have any secrets?' (37.)

Page 26. *'Laure & Lenze'.* No tune or song by this name appears in *Grandison.* Probably *Laura und Lenza* by Cesare Bossi. (See Introduction, pp. 15–16.)

Harpsichord. Charlotte's favourite resort in times of stress: 'I carolled away every care at my harpsichord' (3. 18); and Harriet reports, 'She saunters about, and affects to be diverted by her harpsichord only' (4. 13).

Page 27. *colds.* Grandison 'inquired kindly' about a cold suffered by Harriet (3. 19).

Page 28. *Charge.* Charlotte refers to Harriet as 'my charge' (1. 26).

Lord & Lady L. They have been away for three months visiting Lord

L.'s estates and relatives, and are expected to return soon to their Colnebrook house.

Page 29. *Sister*. Grandison can refer to Harriet as 'our new sister' because she has been welcomed into the keeping of himself and his sister and has become one of the family in a fuller sense than this phrase carries today.

Charlotte reports to Harriet that after meeting her again, following the rescue, Grandison 'did nothing but talk of his new-found sister, from the time he parted with you' (1. 37).

Page 31. *fit*. Meaning mood or inclination, in the colloquial sense of an itch or a yen. This jokey meaning is also in Richardson. Harriet tells Lucy Selby that 'when the fit is upon her' Charlotte 'regards not whether it is a china cup, or a cork, that she pats and tosses about' in order to torment Lord G. (4. 14).

Act 4. Scene 1.

Page 32. Jane Austen follows Richardson in the relationship between Charlotte and Lord G. Charlotte tyrannizes him, treats him contemptuously, and creates situations to insult and humiliate him. Harriet explains it, over-generously, as her 'kittenish disposition . . . for it is not so much the love of power that predominates in her mind, as the love of playfulness'. But she does see that 'her *sport* will certainly be the *death* of Lord G—'s happiness' (4. 14). Grandison describes Lord G. as 'a worthy, though not a very brilliant man' (3. 19); Harriet sees him as 'a modest young man: he is genteel, well-bred' (3. 19). As Richardson draws him, Lord G. is a very recognizable type— one of life's victims, the hen-pecked man who asks for it and unfailingly arouses the spiteful side of other people, as he does here with Charlotte. Both Grandison and Harriet try to intervene on his behalf and tell Charlotte how cruelly she treats him, just as here in the play.

wait. Throughout this scene, Charlotte makes a great deal of Lord G.'s lateness. This probably derives from 4. 37, where Charlotte, now Lady G., to the acute embarrassment of her guests, insists on serving dinner before her husband has returned home.

Have patience. Grandison's intervention, on behalf of Lord G., is in character with the novel, where he promotes Lord G. as the prime candidate for his sister's hand in marriage. Throughout Volume Three, there are a number of set-piece disputes between them on this subject.

Page 33. severe. Harriet charges Charlotte with severity: 'Nay now, Miss Grandison, you are so much more severe upon your sex, and upon matrimony, than Sir Charles' (3. 17).

civillest. Grandison delivers a lecture to his sister on the offensiveness of her witty rudeness and the '*Times* and *Occasions*' when it might and might not be used (3. 16); and extensively again in 3. 17.

Page 34. Lines 2–3. Cf. Grandison's comment: 'he is also a mild man: he will bear a great deal' (3. 19).

liking your wit. Cf. Grandison's reprimand: 'I love to feel the *finer* edge of your wit; But when I was bespeaking your attention upon a very serious subject; a subject that concerned the happiness of your future life, and if *yours*, mine; and you could be able to say something that became only the mouth of an unprincipled woman to say; how could I forbear to wish that some *other* woman, and not my sister, had said it?' (3. 16.)

Emily. Emily Jervois, Grandison's ward.

favourite. Charlotte constantly complains of Grandison's preference for her elder sister: 'Lady L.—has got the start of me in my brother's affections: but she is my elder sister; first come, first served' (2. 5). She admits to it, under the guise of joking: 'I am jealous. Lady L—, don't think to rob me of my Harriet's preferable love, as you have of Sir Charles's. I *will* be best sister here' (2. 2). Harriet reports this to Lucy Selby: that Grandison 'once said, as Miss Grandison told me, that the Countess of L—is still a more excellent woman than my Charlotte' (1. 37).

Lord L. He backs up Grandison in the great reprimand scene in 3. 16.

Page 35. raillery. Grandison refers to that 'vein of raillery, which, when opened, she knows not always how to stop' (3. 19).

Page 37. *Pollexfens*. Grandison is occasionally capable of humour. But one cannot really imagine Richardson's hero making a joke like this about Pollexfen, even with Harriet out of the room.

Page 38. *loving Couple*. Charlotte's sarcastic tone is also in *Grandison*. She writes to Harriet that Lord and Lady L. 'are as fond as apes' (6. 47); and she indulges herself, at some length, when Lady L. confides that she and her husband share a common purse (4. 17).

Page 40. *my turn*. Emily Jervois is stung by Charlotte's comment since she was in love with Grandison and had hoped to marry him.

Page 41. *mind*. Harriet's possession of a mind is emphasized at the novel's beginning, in Letter Two, where Greville writes to Lady Frampton that it is impossible to describe Harriet's beauties by reference to her 'person' alone: 'animated as every feature is by a mind that bespeaks all human excellence, and dignifies her in every air, in every look, in every motion . . . but lovely as Miss Byron's person is, I defy the greatest sensualist on earth not to admire her mind more than her person . . . such a native dignity in all she says, in all she does (though mingled with a frankness that shows her mind's superiority to the minds of almost all other women)'.

Of course, Greville's commendation is highly equivocal. But he says that he is uplifted by Harriet's qualities.

Richardson, in common with many eighteenth-century writers, allowed 'mind' a comprehensive meaning: it was not just the intellectual faculty, but a unity of thinking, feeling, and acting.

happy medium. Again, mentioned in Greville's letter. He remarks on Harriet's combination and balance of qualities: 'a native dignity in all she says, in all she does . . . She jests; she raillies'.

Gravity. Cf. Charlotte's question: 'Yet you are so grave. Were you always such a grave, such a wise, such a *very* wise girl, Harriet?' (2. 6).

offence. Cf. Harriet's comment to Lucy Selby: 'There are not many men, my Lucy, who can make a compliment to one lady, without robbing, or, at least, depreciating another' (2. 1). Unlike Lord G. here, Grandison, of course, does not put his foot in it; and Harriet's comment is inspired by his knack of passing backhand-free compliments.

Act 5. Scene 1.

Page 42. In the novel, Grandison visits Selby House in Northampton-shire to seek the approval of Harriet's closest relatives for his proposal of marriage; and the marriage-terms are the concern of Mr Deane, a lawyer, Harriet's godfather to whom she is 'daughter by adoption' (6. 13).

18. Possibly a private joke for some member of the family or close friend; in *Grandison*, she is twenty.

22. Mr Selby, 'with his usual facetiousness', wants to hurry the marriage: 'I am for sending up for Sir Charles out of hand. Let him come the first day of next week, and let them be married before the end of it' (6. 8); and Grandison himself would like 'an early day' (6. 26).

Mr Selby's objection, here, to an early marriage, may have been borrowed by Jane Austen from a different proposal, Lord L.'s application to Sir Thomas Grandison for Caroline Grandison's hand, which was refused (2. 14).

Page 43. *Clementina.* See Introduction, p. 19.

my objection. Grandison wrote to Clementina (as reported by Mrs Beaumont): 'It became him, he says, in honour, in gratitude, tho' the difficulties in his way seemed insuperable, (And so they *must* seem), to hold himself in suspense, and not to offer to make his addresses to any other woman' (6. 36).

Letters. In 6. 17 Clementina's brother Jeronymo reports that the family hope that they will succeed in persuading her to accept the Count of Belvedere. In 7. 47 we have the last letter from Italy reporting her decision to give herself a year to think this over.

wishes. Clementina links up her desire with a wish to 'be assured of your happiness in marriage with an English, at least not an Italian woman' (5. 35).

Page 44. *prudence.* One of Harriet's striking qualities; not, as in modern English, carrying unattractive overtones of cautiousness and un-adventurousness, but with a strongly positive note of wisdom. It is celebrated by Greville at the beginning of the novel: 'the prudence visible in her whole aspect, gave her a distinction, even at Twelve, that promised what she would be at a riper age' (1. 2). It is a quality that impresses another reprobate, Pollexfen himself: 'such is the opinion I have of your prudence, that I will adopt them [Harriet's 'sentiments'] and make them my own' (1. 17). Mrs Selby indicates that it is a quality for which she is widely admired: 'that prudence for which you have hitherto been so much applauded by every one' (1. 40); and Grandison refers to the importance of her 'prudence' in their own relationship (6. 26).

Page 45. *refused . . . Neighbourhood.* Coming to London, Harriet left behind three strong admirers: Greville, Fenwick, and Orme, who already knew, according to Lucy Selby, 'that you are not inclined to favour any of the three' (1. 1).

no more than 14,000£. Mr Deane writes to Grandison that her fortune 'in her own right, is no more than between Thirteen and Fourteen thousand pounds' (6. 15).

Jewel. Mr Selby describes Harriet as a 'jewel' (1. 24), as do Grandison (1. 28) and Lord W. (6. 51).

double wedding. Charlotte wishes for this: 'Would to heaven that the same hour that my hand and Lord G—'s were joined, yours and my brother's were also united!' (4. 11). But it happens that her marriage occurs first, on 11 April (Volume Four), Harriet's on 15 November (Volume Six).

Page 46. *Adsheart.* Taken direct from the novel: a provincialism, to bring out Mr Selby's downright Northamptonshirism, his lack of urban polish and verbal refinement. Harriet draws attention to it, writing to Grandison: 'My uncle was petulant. *I,* said he, am always in the wrong: you women, never. He ran into all those peculiarities of words, for which you have so often rallied him His *adsheart,* his *female scrupulosities,* his *what a prize . . .*' (6. 17).

plague. Mr Selby has one notable row with his wife (6. 17).

Dame Selby. Another of Mr Selby's countryisms (6. 17, 25).

Act 5. Scene 2.

Page 47. married at home. i.e. rather than in church. The issue is not just one of privacy v. a public, society occasion, as would befit such a marriage. A church marriage was thought to be more sacred, more spiritually committing, than a ceremony conducted in the privacy of the home. Harriet reports the great debate on this question in 4. 14: 'Charlotte, the perverse Charlotte, insisted on not going to church', her reason, half-joking, that a vow of obedience made in a 'chamber' would weigh less heavily upon her.

As it happens the question is not put directly to Grandison, although, according to Dr Bartlett, he would be against it, and Charlotte gives in: 'Do as you will—or, rather, as my brother will— What signifies opposing *him*?'; and it is agreed that her wedding 'shall be solemnised, as privately as possible, at St. George's Church' (4. 15). Richardson was here touching upon a question of considerable contemporary importance. Until the Marriage Bill of 1753, secret marriages performed by an ordained minister were legal; hence Pollexfen's attempt. The Bill established that a valid marriage could only be performed by a minister of the Church of England in the parish church after the banns had been read there on three successive Sundays, and with an official licence. The significance of this in Richardson's fiction is discussed by Ian Watt, *The Rise of the Novel* (1957), pp. 149–51, where he mentions the controversy that also arose over the publicity and ceremonial that now attended the marriage service.

Page 48. few people be by. Harriet would prefer a private church wedding: 'I should wish to have it as private as possible.' But Mr Selby organizes a day of public ceremony and rejoicing so that the family can share their happiness with the 'neighbours and tenants . . . no *hugger-hugger* doings—let private weddings be for *doubtful* happiness—' (6. 44). This issue arises again when Harriet asks Charlotte why Grandison agreed to this arrangement (6. 51).

Page 49. Marmouset. This joke on Mrs Reeves's baby sounds rather more fierce than it really is: it was the eighteenth-century equivalent of the affectionate 'you little monkey'.

Charlotte calls her own baby a 'marmouset' (7. 47), 'pug' (7. 47), and 'brat' (7. 52).

George Eliot was very taken by this side of Charlotte. While she found Harriet unlikeable, 'too proper and insipid', 'Lady G. is the gem, with her marmoset' (Letter to Bessie Parkes, 30 October 1852).